MOVED TO TEARS, MOVED TO ACTION

MOVED TO TEARS, MOVED TO ACTION

Solution focused brief therapy with women and children

Jane Lethem

BT Press

First published January 1994
Published by BT Press
17 Avenue Mansions, Finchley Road, London NW3 7AX

© Jane Lethem 1994

Set by Alex Gollner

ISBN 1 871697 68 9

Contents

Jane Lethem read Experimental Psychology at Oxford and trained in Clinical Psychology in Liverpool, where she first developed an interest in family therapy. Since qualifying she has worked for the National Health Service, in Oxford and London, specializing in work with children, adolescents and families. She is currently employed by the North West London Mental Health N.H.S. Trust and is an Honourary Lecturer in Psychology at University College London.

Her involvement in Brief Therapy began in the mid 80s, initially influenced by the Problem Focused approach of the Mental Research Institute, California, where she studied. Since joining the Brief Therapy Project, based at the Marlborough Family Service, London, in 1990, her clinical work, writing and teaching have moved increasingly toward a Solution Focused approach. In 1993 she joined the Brief Therapy Practice.

Acknowledgments

This book makes reference to many therapists, writers and researchers who have influenced me. I would like to acknowledge in a more personal way a number of people who have helped me in the work which formed the basis for the book.

Firstly, I would like to express my gratitude to all the clients whose stories, somewhat disguised, appear in the following pages.

I would like to thank Dr. John Green who has supported the development of my special interest in Solution Focused Brief Therapy. I owe a great deal to Evan George, Chris Iveson, Harvey Ratner, and Ann Stevens for making Wednesday afternoons in the Brief Therapy Project the high point of my working week, and for their encouragement at every stage of the production of the book. Special thanks to Evan for his thoughtful comments on the penultimate draft. I very much appreciate the contribution of Esther Bloch, Sophia Goddard, Jill Jenkins, Dr. Helen Likierman, Ilona McDowell, Diane Melvin, Ann Miller, Dr. Wendy Stayte, Michele Sullivan and Haidi Totsika, to constructive discussions of drafts of various chapters. Charlotte Burck, Dr. Alan Cooklin, Jan Cooper and Bebe Speed deserve special thanks for challenging comments and debate about Solution Focused Brief Therapy which, I believe, have helped to sharpen some of my ideas. Finally, I am grateful to Richard Gollner for taking a commendably solution focused attitude to encouraging me to write this book, persistently helping me to identify the next small step toward completing it.

J.L.

Introduction
"It looks different when you do it"

A female family therapist who had observed my work commented that Solution Focused Brief Therapy looked different when being done by a woman and that the experience had overcome some of her reservations about the approach. I assumed she was referring to a comparatively rare opportunity to observe a female role model and that different features of the method had been highlighted when watching a female therapist in contrast to those she may have noticed when watching a male therapist or hearing a male exponent of the approach. I am not exactly sure what she meant and, in retrospect, I wish that I had asked at the time. I have been preoccupied since then by the issues raised by her comment, issues concerning women as therapists and clients of an approach which I have found inspiring.

Solution Focused Brief Therapy emphasizes clients' talents, resources, and existing problem-solving abilities. It is goal directed and generally more concerned with the present and future than with the past. The principles of the approach are as relevant to supervision and consultation as they are to therapy and counselling. Although some aspects of solution focused work, illustrated in the chapters which follow, should be familiar to any therapist or counsellor, its underlying assumptions challenge many of those associated with other processes designed to help individuals and families who are experiencing problems.

Women are the major consumers of mental health services[1] and the majority of those practising counselling are female[2]. The reasons for these gender imbalances are complex, some representing constraints upon women, some suggesting helpful opportunities for them. Definitions of mental health remain predominantly defined by men[3] with different criteria being used for men and women to be judged in need of help, making it likely that more women than men will be advised to seek help, either for themselves or for their children. The special stresses on women[4] may make more of them experience a need for help. The fact that women are socialized to develop sensitivity to the feelings of others and to take responsibility for making relationships work[5] leads to therapy or counselling appearing a more 'natural' activity for both clients and therapists who are women.

Personal problems, family problems, and couple problems have a way of colouring individuals' views of themselves, and of leading to preoccupation with failure, helplessness or self-blame. Many clients arrive for therapy feeling little more than "a case for treatment", rather than a whole person, and expect to be labelled and even blamed by the therapist. This is especially so for women, accustomed as they are to looking after relationships. As one female client said of herself, "Isn't it usually the mother's fault?"

Most of my colleagues in the National Health Service are women; most of my clients are women, young people or children. Since 1984 I have been involved in developing and sharing in the provision of clinical psychology services for children and adolescents and their families in two inner London districts, a process which has confronted me daily with the injustices faced by women raising or caring for children, especially those coping with financial hardship, violence in the home and/or racism. My work has brought me into contact with largely female staff groups in day nurseries and children's health clinics as well as with many women raising children as single parents. The expectation of blame and a sense of embittered helplessness have often been strong themes in the accounts both mothers and carers give of their attempts to meet the emotional needs of children and to cope with problems which arise.

My therapeutic orientation has shifted over this time, from Cognitive-Behavioural[6] and Problem Focused Brief Therapy[7] approaches to a greater emphasis on Solution Focused Brief Therapy. However, there has been a common strand running through my contact with children, parents and carers, that of the need to recognize and find ways to make explicit the contribution of social injustice to the problems for which psychological help was being sought. In this respect, I have shared concerns which preoccupy many feminists, attempting to find common ground between beliefs about social justice and therapy, and those therapists and counsellors who have been trying to make their therapy more gender aware and racially aware.

I have found some liberating and helpful ideas in the Brief Therapy literature, the sources of which I shall go into in more detail in the chapters which follow. Firstly there is an emphasis on ways of revealing and affirming the strengths of clients who may have been feeling helpless. Secondly, the framework offers scope, if the therapist and client wish to take the opportunity, to develop a narrative about the client's past, present and future which includes issues of gender, sexual orientation, race and class.

In 1986 I spent a month participating in the residency programme of the Mental Research Institute (M.R.I.) in Palo Alto, California. I spent as much time as possible with the members of M.R.I.'s Brief Therapy Center. During my stay, I attended a workshop entitled 'Brief Therapy with Women' given by Phyllis Nauts, an M.R.I. trained therapist[8].

She was the first person to draw my attention to the special value for women, and also children, of approaches which celebrate achievements which have been taken for granted. The accomplishments of women or children may seem modest unless account is taken of the adverse circumstances in which they have occurred. She highlighted the need to clarify those aspects of the client's life which are within and those which are outside the client's control. For example, the final decision about a single parent's housing may lie with an official of the local council and may not reflect the extent to which the family needs or deserves housing. A therapist should acknowledge both the adverse effects upon family life of poor accommodation and the fact that the family is in no way to blame for inadequate municipal housing. The therapist and client may then go on to discuss aspects of family life over which the client has an influence, thereby enabling the mother to clarify those things she is already doing for herself and her children and those she would like to do, wherever they live. The therapist might also explore with her whether she has done all that she would like to do to try to influence the official's decision. "Empowerment", her term for this process, was novel to me at the time. I found her ideas helpful in answering the question "What has therapy got to offer those whose problems are largely the result of social injustice?"

In 1989 Harvey Ratner, Social Worker at the Marlborough Family Service in London, telephoned me. He had been in California on holiday staying with relatives and had visited the M.R.I. After a stimulating day talking with Richard Fisch, the Director of the Brief Therapy

Center, and Karin Schlanger, a member of that team, Harvey asked whether they had many British visitors. They replied that there had been few but that a British woman who had completed a month's residency with them in 1986 had written quite recently to say she had moved job to St. Mary's Hospital in London. Her name, you can guess. St. Mary's and the Marlborough Family Service are about a mile apart.

On his return to Britain, Harvey invited me to visit the Brief Therapy Project, based at the Marlborough Family Service. I met Harvey and his colleagues Ann Stevens, Evan George and Chris Iveson, and observed their work together one Wednesday afternoon. The visit quickly led to an invitation to join the Brief Therapy Project. Change can happen quickly with the right catalyst. Thank you, Dick and Karin. I was welcomed both as a potentially like-minded therapist and as another woman for a team which needed to become more balanced in terms of gender.

The Brief Therapy Project exists as one of a number of specialist projects within The Marlborough Family Service, a multi-disciplinary mental health facility which offers a range of outpatient and day patient services for children, adolescents, and adults. The Project started with the aim of putting the ideas of Steve de Shazer[9,10,11] and colleagues of the Brief Therapy Center, Milwaukee, into practice in a multi-cultural inner London context[12].

During the course of working together, we have also been influenced and frequently encouraged by the work of other therapists, referred to in later chapters, as well as by colleagues, most notably Saleha Islam, who joined the Project temporarily during her Social Work training. Although de Shazer's model of therapy does not address differences of gender, race, class or sexuality directly, these were already issues of concern to each of us, prior to the setting up of the Project. Along with many Health and Social Services professionals, we had a growing awareness of our responsibility to recognize the deleterious effects on mental health of inequalities associated with such differences and to incorporate a sensitivity to differences, in staff as well as clients, into our work.

In 1989, Chris Iveson, Evan George and Harvey Ratner, with the assistance of Richard Gollner, set up The Brief Therapy Practice. This is a freelance organization which provides teaching and consultation in

Solution Focused Brief Therapy. As well as hosting presentations by internationally known brief therapists, the founder members participated in a nationwide programme of workshops and consultations. It expanded in 1993 when Di Iveson and I joined the Practice. To date it has taught in excess of 3,000 therapists and counsellors to at least an introductory level in the approach.

This volume concentrates on my own experience of the way our ideas and practices have evolved with special reference to issues which affect women and children. Chapter 1 is intended as an introduction to, or reminder of, the theory and practice of Solution Focused Brief Therapy together with an outline of developments within the Brief Therapy Project. In Chapter 2, I state the advantages, as I see them, of the approach for women clients and therapists and for therapists of either gender who wish to bring a sensitivity to gender to their work. Chapters 3 to 6 concern particular client groups: single parent mothers, children, clients who have been sexually abused in childhood, and clients with experience of violence in the home.

The groupings are somewhat arbitrary as Solution Focused Brief Therapy does not categorize clients on the basis of problems or demographic details. The issues covered are far from comprehensive but reflect the client groups with which I do most of my work: children, adolescents and their families. Older women are largely missing from the following pages until my mother and grandmother make fleeting appearances in Chapter 8. The majority of my women clients have children who are still at home. However there are a number of examples of therapy with single women who live alone. The names and some personal details of clients have been changed to protect confidentiality.

Chapter 7 is a reflection on my experience as "my female colleague", consulting to male colleagues. It outlines my perspective on the development of the Brief Therapy Project. Chapter 8 seeks to celebrate therapists' individual qualities in the practice of Solution Focused Brief Therapy.

Chapter 1
Solution Focused Theory and Practice

Solution Focused Brief Therapy, pioneered by de Shazer[9,10,11] and colleagues who included Insoo Kim Berg[13], Eve Lipchik[14], and Michele Weiner-Davis[15,20] concentrates on clients' strengths, including their capacities to imagine and specify goals for change. It facilitates their recognition of their successes, however small, in coping with and gradually resolving problems, with a view to building upon these existing solutions. For therapists who are willing to apply the same principles to themselves, the approach has the potential to mobilize the individual qualities and strengths of the therapist too. Although this approach, and the related Brief Problem Focused approach of the Mental Research Institute (M.R.I.)[16,17] which pre-dated it, were not developed with any specific client group in mind, they have a special value for clients who feel they have little control over their own lives.

The Family Tree of Brief Therapies

Some solution focused practitioners now eschew the definition 'systemic', however, the Problem Focused and Solution Focused Brief Therapies have their roots in systems theory. The founding figures of the problem focused approach, John Weakland, Paul Watzlawick, and Richard Fisch, developed their ideas out of early research projects initiated by Gregory Bateson, and were influenced by Milton H. Erikson's therapy[18] and Heinz von Foerster's ideas about constructivism[19]. Whilst diametrically opposite in emphasis, the solution focused approach shares many of the assumptions with those of the M.R.I. Both specifically require the therapist to explore and show respect for clients' values and theories about themselves, and to help them to identify concrete goals for change. Both emphasize the significance of small changes and encourage clients to identify the next small step toward problem resolution which they would like to take. The possibility of rapid resolution of problems is highlighted in both methods.

In the wider context outside Britain, other key players in this burgeoning field of therapies include, in the U.S.: Bill O'Hanlon, who terms his approach Solution Oriented Therapy[20,21,22], and Yvonne Dolan, who employs Ericksonian and Solution Focused Therapy with survivors of child sexual abuse[23]. M.R.I.'s second generation of brief therapists includes: Pat Emard, Lyn Jordan, who has put brief therapy ideas into practice in a field social work context with "reluctant clients"[24], and Karin Schlanger. Ben Furman and Tapani Ahola in Finland conduct Solution Talk[25] with clients, together with groups of colleagues. In Australia and New Zealand, Michael White and David Epston[26,27] have drawn on Michel Foucault's philosophy[28] and anthropological sources including the work of Clifford Geertz[29,30] in developing a narrative approach. Brian Cade[22] and Michael Durrant[31] are family therapists who have moved in an increasingly solution focused direction. Kiwi Tamase, Warihi Campbell, Charles Waldegrave[32], and colleagues drawn from Pacific Island, Maori and White New Zealand cultures, practice Just Therapy, which takes into account the gender, cultural, social and economic context of the person seeking help. They have structured their team work to enable all therapists working with female clients to be accountable to the women in the team, all the work with any one of the ethnic groups to be accountable to therapists from the same ethnic group.

The Brief Therapy Project, London

We spend one afternoon each week working together, seeing cases drawn from the children, young people, and adults referred to the Marlborough Family Service in London. One-way screens and video recording facilities are available. While one therapist, if necessary with an interpreter, interviews the client(s), one or more of the other members of the Project act as a consultation team, usually observing behind the one-way screen. The Project attracts visitors from the mental health professions, many from abroad. They can, with clients' permission, join the team. Clients are encouraged to meet the team if they wish.

Women clients who are known to have experienced sexual abuse or violence by men are generally seen by a female therapist and requests, by clients, for a therapist of the same gender are respected. We draw on our own differences in family background, religion and gender when consulting with one another. Although we use de Shazer's framework for therapy, our practice has been shaped by our own values, experiences with clients and the influence of other members of the 'family tree of brief therapists'.

Conversations about solutions

The style of communication is conversational once the formality of explaining the one way screen and, if appropriate, seeking permission to videotape is over. There is no taboo about a degree of self-disclosure by the therapist and the emphasis is on cooperation rather than confrontation. The first part of any therapeutic conversation is usually taken up with 'problem free talk'. Therapists ask clients about general aspects of their lives, for example their homes, schools, jobs, recreational activities and interests, with the accent on aspects with which clients are satisfied and about which they feel competent and confident. Thus from the outset, the client is treated as a whole person, rather than just a person with a problem. Clients have the experience of spending part of therapy recalling and discussing 'problem free' facets of their lives which are likely to be of relevance to developing solutions to the problems which have brought them to therapy.

The problem and the past

Our approach is largely future oriented. We assume that understanding why a problem began and how it developed over time is not a necessary part of solution development. We believe it is more important to explore where clients want to get to than where they have come from. While de Shazer would usually interrupt what he terms 'problem talk', for instance detailed descriptions of the client's problem, we have found that some clients feel that the therapist can only understand their predicament fully by hearing about the problem and its history.

Although it would, theoretically, be possible to conduct Solution Focused Brief Therapy without knowing any details of the problem, compassion and the wish to establish rapport lead us to listen attentively to what clients want us to hear. However, if a conversation appears likely to become dominated by problem descriptions, complaints or expressions of distress, we usually attempt to acknowledge the client's feelings and then ask "Is talking in this way helpful, or are there other things you would like to concentrate on as well today?"

Some clients let us know that the opportunity to talk about problems is important and helpful, others welcome the opportunity to review their purpose in coming to therapy that day and wish to change the topic to one which is more beneficial to them. While avoiding interrupting clients, we look for opportunities to begin asking about exceptions to the problem and hoped for improvements. When clients appear preoccupied by the past, the therapist can take the opportunity to ask about past coping, and sources of help and comfort, as well as hearing about past trauma. Problems are not seen as pathological, but as aspects of life from which clients would like to move on or with which they would like to cope differently.

Change before therapy

We ask clients early in our first meeting about any 'pre-session changes' in their lives, especially in relation to the problem, that have occurred recently. Michele Weiner Davis's research[33] demonstrated that a significant number of clients make important changes in their lives between seeking and taking up therapy. When clients feel in a rut it is helpful to ask them to pay attention to change. Whenever possible, at the time of offering an appointment, we ask clients to notice any changes in their lives between then and keeping the appointment, explaining that we will be interested to ask them about their observations. It is not unusual for clients to report significant improvements in the area for which they are seeking help or active attempts to find new solutions to their problems.

Solutions

We devote as much time as possible in conversation with clients to talking about solutions: past successes in solving or coping with problems; current partial solutions to the problems which have brought them to therapy and possible ways to amplify these successful actions in the future.

Exceptions

However entrenched and all-pervasive a difficulty may seem, there are always exceptions, that is, times when the problem is absent or less severe. Some may emerge when the therapist asks the client what changes have occurred prior to the session or during the 'problem free' part of the conversation, others by specific enquiries which should be worded carefully. Clients frequently feel that a problem is watertight and if asked "Are there ever any times when the problem is absent or less severe?" are likely automatically to respond "No". There are always exceptions to any predicament and the therapist's questions should reflect the expectation of uncovering these. Examples are given below:

"When does your daughter listen to you?"

"What is different about the times you *resist* the temptation to binge?"

"When you are feeling *happier*, what do you find yourself doing?"

"What has been your longest period of *abstinence* from drinking?"

"In which situations *do* you keep your temper?"

"Tell me about the last time you *did* manage to get out of the house?"

"What things have you found to do that help you to be *less* anxious sometimes?"

"What is the *closest* your son has got to using the lavatory properly?"

"When was the last time your mother *did* show some respect for your wishes?"

"What has *helped* that loving feeling to develop?"

"What have you found helps to keep the craving for drugs a little more *under control?*"

Discussing examples of occasions on which the difficulty has not occurred as expected, or situations in which the client knows the problem will not occur, provide vital clues to successful resolution of the problem. The client's view of the obstacle begins to be deconstructed while successful aspects of life on which to build are illuminated. De Shazer quotes the American adage "If it ain't broke, don't fix it". Clients are usually doing many successful things to facilitate exceptions and to solve their own problems and therapy offers the chance to recognize and continue these. Ideally, unsuccessful approaches should be discontinued. Utilization of a client's existing ways of solving and/or coping with a problem may be considered more respectful, less intrusive and more economical, than the suggestion by the therapist of new solutions.

Change: client's choice of direction

Some assumptions are shared with other systemic approaches to therapy, for example that change, in some form, is constant and inevitable, that a small change can have far-reaching effects setting in motion the resolution of a problem and that change in one part of a system can lead to change in the system as a whole. However, the choice of the direction of change belongs to the client. The therapist assists by helping to identify and clarify goals. The nature of the power imbalance between client and therapist is explicit; therapists put their skills at the disposal of clients who have the choice of the aims of their therapy. Thus each client has his or her own way of cooperating with the therapist whose task is that of exploring the form that cooperation takes rather than making the attribution of 'resistance' at times when therapy is difficult for the therapist[34]. It is not essential to see all members of a family, but to bear them in mind while working with the most motivated member.

Brevity

We feel that therapy should take as few sessions as are necessary because, in our view, there is no intrinsic value in being in therapy; it is for the purpose of helping clients to reach their chosen goals. Depending upon the nature of their objectives, some clients may be seen over comparatively long periods of time, usually at infrequent intervals.

Goals

The approach is explicitly purposeful. Within legal and ethical limits, the client may select goals that have little in common with the motivation of the referrer. For example, the parents of a child on the Child Protection Register may have the aim of ridding themselves of contact with Social Services. This opens up the possibility of a conversation between the therapist and the parents about the kind of observable changes they think a Social Worker would want to see in their family before being willing to recommend removal of their child from the Register and the eventual ending of the involvement of Social Services in their lives.

Some clients can readily answer the question "How will you know when you have no further need for therapy?", others need a lot of assistance in identifying and clarifying their objectives. The clearer, more specific and more realistic the goal, the better is the client's chance of reaching it. The 'miracle question' is often used to help clients to imagine a problem-free future and to provide details of their aspirations:

"Suppose that tonight, while you are sleeping, a miracle occurs, and the problem that brought you to therapy is suddenly resolved. The miracle occurs while you are sleeping so you do not immediately know that it has happened. When you wake up, what is the first thing that you will notice that will let you know that there has been a miracle?"[10]

Step by step

Goals, even those that are clear and defined in concrete terms, can seem very far away. Identifying the next step, however small, that clients can take to help themselves to move in their chosen direction helps to make the process achievable. A scale, from 0 to 10, may be used to clarify how far along that path the client has already come, how much further there is to go and what the signs will be of progress to the next point on the scale. When clients have reached their objectives and give a rating of 10, or whatever level they feel is acceptable, they may be unsure whether the improvement can be maintained. In such cases, asking for an additional rating, of confidence in staying at 10, or the number with which they are satisfied, may be illuminating. Children may need a pictorial representation of a scale, for example, steps on a ladder or stepping stones, to assist them in answering scaling questions.

"Is there anything else you would like to say?"

We are aware that some clients come to see a therapist not only for therapy but in the hope of obtaining protection from danger or the opportunity to make a disclosure about physical or sexual abuse. When teaching workshops, one of the most frequent questions asked is "If you concentrate on problem-free talk and exceptions, how do clients who want to tell you about being abused get the chance to do so?". I have even been asked whether I have such a personal aversion to hearing about painful experiences that I effectively silence my clients on such issues.

As should be clear from the examples in later chapters concerning violence and child sexual abuse, clients do make disclosures to therapists who work in a solution focused way. We have the impression that the atmosphere created in solution focused sessions does not put clients under pressure and enables them to say what they wish in their own time. There have been a number of clients who, having reached their initial goals of therapy, have then asked for further help, in coping with the long term effects of childhood abuse which they have not disclosed to anyone before. To ensure that clients have the space in which to raise any issues they wish, we have developed the habit of regularly asking "Is there anything else you would like to say?", "Is there anything else you would like me to know?" or "Is there anything you have not yet had the chance to tell me, that you wish to?"

As with any form of therapy, if a client's reply to such questions leads the therapist to believe that a child may be at risk of any form of abuse, then therapy must take second place to child protection. For example, in the closing minutes of an interview with an Afro-Caribbean family, mother Anita, stepfather Sam and child Robert, focusing on Anita's gradual success in making satisfactory access arrangements with her six year old son's biological father, each member of the family was asked if they had anything else they wanted to say. When Robert's turn came he told the therapist that Sam had beaten him. After hearing details of the event from the child and the stepfather, the therapist decided that the child's safety could be at risk and informed the local Social Services who put their Child Protection procedure into effect. As is usual in such situations, the therapist felt some regret at the deleterious effect upon the therapeutic relationship with the family but recognized that therapy could be of little benefit if the child continued to be at risk of physical abuse.

Consultation break
During the interview the team pays particular attention to the client's strengths, successful attempts at finding solutions for problems and motivation for change. With the exception of comparatively rare occasions when unexpected disclosures, like the one above, are made, these observations by the team will form the basis for feedback by the therapist to the client(s). Visitors to the project are encouraged to notice those aspects of the interview and participate in generating feedback for the therapist to share with the client. Occasionally, a reflecting team[35] may be used, with client(s) and therapist observing the consultation team as they discuss the conversation they have heard.

Feedback

Most of the feedback is taken up with compliments concerning the client's personal qualities, efforts at self-help, coping, or determination to reach a resolution, whichever is appropriate. Compliments are usually set in the context of the challenges facing the client which may include social injustice as well as emotional stress. The problem and the client's attempts at solving it may be described in terms of the development of the individual or of the family life cycle.

Encouragement is given to continue activities that have been found to be successful in tackling or coping with the problem. Unhelpful activities may either be ignored in the feedback or gently discouraged, in favour of "doing something different", the choice of different activity being left to the client. Clients may be given the task of noticing something in the days to come before the next appointment, for example, "Notice those things you do that help you to keep at your rating of 5, and pay attention to any signs that at times you are reaching 6" or "Notice those things in your life that you want to continue". Sometimes the atmosphere during feedback can be light and celebratory, 'cheering on change'[36]. At other times, when a client has been distressed or particularly emotionally vulnerable during the session, the therapist must acknowledge those feelings while giving compliments.

Working without a team

A team is not essential. When working alone, taking a break can be particularly helpful to enable therapists/counsellors to have a few quiet minutes to reflect on the conversation and to select suitable compliments to feed back to their clients. Clients also appear to benefit from the opportunity to review the conversation and prepare to listen attentively to the feedback.

Chapter 2
The lens of gender

Solution Focused Brief Therapy is currently practised by both male and female therapists with men, women and children clients, seen individually, in couples and families. Gender has not been an overt issue for the founders of the approach. However, the most prominent figures in its development and teaching have been male and there is some controversy over whether it may be considered equally sensitive to the needs of male and female clients.

As a practical person and a psychologist accustomed to negotiating the goals of therapy with my clients whenever possible, Solution Focused work appealed to me initially because of its emphasis on enabling clients to specify clear and concrete goals which take into account their interactions with significant others. I like a therapeutic contract in which both client and therapist know when their work together has been completed. The more I have studied it and used it and the more I have reflected upon the observation "It looks different when you do it", the more I have come to recognize Solution Focused Brief Therapy's special congruence for women, as summarized in points 1 to 6 below.

1. Conversational communication
Much of each therapy session is taken up with informal 'problem-free talk', mutual self disclosure between client and therapist and the development of a cooperative attitude to discussing the aims of the meeting. Thus the prevailing mode of communication reflects a style of interaction in which most women are experienced and competent[37].

2. Exoticising the domestic
Exploration of presession change, problem-free aspects of the client's life, exceptions and existing solutions illuminates assets which the client may have overlooked, a process White has called 'exoticising the domestic'[38] and which I believe to be of particular value in reassessing 'women's work'.

For example, Sonia, a single parent mother of Afro-Caribbean descent whose only child, Jerome, had been referred because of disruptive behaviour at school and at home, told the therapist that the day before the appointment, she had decided to visit the child's school and that she and the child's teacher had decided together on some consistent sanctions for unacceptable behaviour and agreed to meet regularly to compare perspectives on Jerome's behaviour. Had the therapist failed to ask "What changes have there been between receiving the appointment and coming to see me today?" Sonia's courage in deciding to approach the school and her success in a delicate negotiation with her child's teacher, by whom she had expected to be blamed, might have been overlooked by both client and therapist.

Another client, Angie, a young white British woman referred because of depression which was thought to be related to her childhood experience of sexual abuse had, between receiving the appointment and attending her first session, moved home, experienced major changes at work and ceased contact with some acquaintances by whom she felt she had been exploited. She initially construed these events as coincidental and insignificant until she and the therapist discussed in detail the ways in which the various changes had come about. Most had involved active steps by Angie who responded favourably when the therapist expressed the view that her role in bringing about the changes in her own life illustrated a capacity, at times, to make decisions, to take control, and to protect herself. These characteristics were all highly relevant to her wish to recover from the long term effects of abuse and remarkable in someone who at times had felt slowed down by depression.

3. Extending the range of contexts

It is customary for the therapist to relate clients' efforts to resolve particular problems to their stage of development as individuals or within families and to highlight any special challenges they have faced. The therapist can extend the range of contexts to describe the client's actions or feelings in relation to inequalities of gender within the family and society, or with reference to other social injustices. For example a single parent mother, Sara, whose family, of black African origin, were refugees, and whose eldest child, Peter, had been referred

for help with emotional adjustment, was complimented for her willingness to meet with the therapist for her son's sake, despite the humil-
iating reception she had received, as a black woman, from many of
the professionals she and her family had encountered in their quest for
a safe place to live.

Rose, an Afro-Caribbean woman in her mid-forties, seemed almost
apologetic when describing to her therapist the distress she had experienced when a close woman friend had left the country permanently.
Rose lived on her own and had, since her divorce, devoted her energies
to her career and friendships. The therapist expressed sympathy with
Rose's grief at the loss of contact with a much loved friend and
attempted to put the meaning of the loss in context. The therapist
pointed out the relative lack of value placed upon friendships between
adults in a society which emphasizes connections between family members and between hetero-sexual partners at the expense of any other
kind of relationship. In such a society, a woman in Rose's position
might feel that she had to apologize for her strong feelings about her
friend's departure rather than expect to receive the kind of support and
understanding that the loss of a family member might have incurred.
For many single people, their closest bonds are with friends and the loss
of a friend deeply affecting.

4. Explicit power imbalance

There is always an imbalance of power between client and therapist in
any form of therapy. Solution Focused therapy, like other co-construc-
tive[39] approaches, minimizes this power differential and makes it overt;
there is an absence of therapeutic mystique. Clients are free to ask therapists about the method and therapists free to answer, although it
should be recognized that clients will vary in their willingness to do this
and will find some therapists more approachable than others. The
therapist has expertise in questioning and discussion about areas of
strength in clients' lives, their aims in coming for therapy and ways of
building on their existing successes in resolving problems. Client are
the experts on their own lives and aspirations and have responsibility
for choosing the direction in which they wish their lives to change and,
if they want, for taking the action required to fulfil their wishes. As
Saleha Islam observed, therapists work very hard in each session but

their responsibility ends at the end of that conversation; it is less tempting to take work preoccupations home when working in this way.

5. Reflexivity
Solution focused ideas may be applied to therapists' work and have the potential to be helpful when therapists are feeling stuck, for example feeling that a conversation is going around in circles, noticing that the client tends to ignore certain kinds of questions or talks mainly about feelings or the past. The overriding principle, that if an activity is successful in resolving a problem, then one should do more of it, if it is not working, then one should do something different, can be applied to the activity of the therapist and may lead to unconventional conversations which do justice to the client's individuality.

6. Reauthoring
Clients frequently come for therapy burdened with descriptions of their lives which emphasize failure, victimization and self blame, narratives influenced by society's prevailing values and prejudices, many of which are misogynistic. Solution focused conversations open up the possibility of clients reauthoring alternative versions of their stories which draw attention to strengths, resources, coping, survival and achievement in the face of adversity and injustice.

For example, Shahina, an Asian woman in her late twenties, who lived with her husband, two children and husband's parents, saw a therapist with her five year old son, Jamal, following referral by the school doctor who felt she needed help "controlling" her child. She saw the referral as shaming and felt anxious about what she considered were her inadequacies as a mother, especially her own lack of formal education. During the conversation with the therapist about Shahina's experience of raising her children in a culture in which racism was a challenge to her family, a picture emerged of a mother who had succeeded in teaching her children to be bilingual, who spoke good English herself, was interested in using her interpreting skills in the local community and who was encouraging her children to cope with two cultures. It was the picture of a woman who had experience of success in raising her children upon which to draw when facing the challenge of Jamal's demanding behaviour in public, and of a son who had already learnt much from his mother and could be expected to respond to her guidance in the present stage of his development.

Problems, dilemmas and solutions

The contrasting ways in which men and women tend to define solutions to dilemmas, men emphasizing logic and abstraction, women concentrating more on the relevance of relationships and the likely emotional consequences of decisions, has been described by Carol Gilligan[40]. Charlotte Burck and Gwyn Daniel[41] have argued that problem-solving approaches to therapy which actively discourage emotional exploration place female clients at a disadvantage. It may be argued that Solution Focused Brief Therapy is likely to be comparatively appealing to men, in view of it's logical step by step approach toward goals with which men might be expected to feel comfortable. This perspective ignores the features of the approach, outlined above, which may draw women to it and overlooks the method's potential for addressing emotional issues in a creative way, acknowledging both the tears and the desire for action.

The miracle question: from tears to action

We find that certain questions can help the client, whether female or male, to describe their imagined miracle in concrete detail, including its social and interactional context. We ask clients to elucidate for us goals concerned with a change in feelings or relationships by asking what observable changes would accompany the experiential change for which they hope. For example:

"What will you find yourself doing that will be a sign of the miracle?"

"How will you know when you are feeling better? What will the first person to notice you are feeling better be able to see to let them know?"

"Who will be the first person to become aware of the miracle?"

"What will your partner, parent, child, colleague, teacher, neighbour, local shop keeper or pet observe you doing that will give them a clue about the miracle?"

"If your miracle involves someone else changing, how will you find yourself behaving once the changes have taken place?"

Anna, a single white European woman in her early twenties, was experiencing difficulty coping following a number of severe stresses over the previous year, related to her health, relationships and employment. She said that after the miracle she "would feel back on course". Further questioning attempted to flesh out an apparently abstract objective.

Therapist What would you see yourself doing when you were back on course?

Client I'd get up in the morning with a purpose, feel happier, go to work, phone my friends, meet people, not feel bored, go out more.. the cinema, have plans for the future, have more hope.

Therapist What difference would it make to your parents?

Client They would feel better because I'd be putting less pressure on them. I'd have occasional contact with them and I'd be minding what my mother says less.

Therapist What would your closest friends notice?

Client That I'd be more positive, I'd be doing something with my work outside 9 to 5, I'd be doing interesting things, travelling again - Europe, I wouldn't be bursting out crying and saying "Why, why, why?" all the time.

Therapist How will you be looking at the past after the miracle?

Client Saying "O.K., it was not all my fault", remembering some of the good things, accepting how it was. I'd know I couldn't change it and can't change it... come to terms with it...

Therapist How would you be looking after your health after the miracle?

Client I'd have more strength, less stress, I'd take my medication [for a medical condition], eat correctly, look after my skin properly.

A scaling question was used with Anna (above).

Therapist You've had a lot to cope with. Let's think back to the time when things were at rock bottom, and call that 0, and let's call after the miracle, when you are 'on course' again, 10. Where would you say you are at the moment ?

Client 4. Some days I can be at 6, then I go down to 4 or 3. Last night I felt... no hope. One person letting me down sets me back.

Therapist It is understandable that setbacks can occur and knock you back a bit. What interests me is what keeps you able to reach 3. What got you from 0 to 3 ?

Client I realized that some friends care, that I have a place to stay and...

I organized my papers... I'm trying to take one step at a time.

Anna's skill in paperwork developed into an important way of getting her life on course, by making lists of necessary actions, setting priorities, and gradually putting some important communications down on paper, including letters to two individuals with whom she had had conflicts which had proved impossible to resolve by other means.

Flexibility

Is Solution Focused Brief Therapy yet another example of an essentially patriarchal perspective misapplied to women, or does it have something special to offer women clients and therapists? In my view, the approach has sufficient flexibility for clients of any age or gender to feel that the therapist is "speaking their language" at least some of the time and has a great deal of potential for therapists who wish to work in a gender-sensitive way. It offers the possibility of logical, practical solution building for which men in general show some preference; it emphasizes concrete descriptions of behaviour which are likely to enable young children to understand what is going on and to participate in therapy; it has the capacity to validate the experiences of women, acknowledge the contribution of social injustice to many of their difficulties and offer them opportunities to utilize strengths they may have overlooked in resolving problems and dilemmas. Although the facets of the approach which make it adaptable with respect to gender are potentially available to both male and female therapists, much is to be learned from female practitioners of Solution Focused Brief Therapy about why "it looks different when (we) do it".

Chapter 3
A woman at the head of the family

There are numerous ways for women to become 'single', 'solo' or 'lone' parents, either temporarily or permanently. They may be on their own for all but the conception of a child or may become the sole carers of children after years of sharing the raising of a family with a partner. Their children may have been unplanned and unwanted, unplanned and wanted or planned and wanted. Single parenting may represent an active choice, a compromise or an unwelcome and unhappy situation.

The circumstances of separation from a partner may range through desertion, escape from a violent partner, mutually agreed parting, divorce, death, and imprisonment. However, women deemed single parents through the lack of a male partner in their lives may not be the sole carers of children. Members of a mother's family of origin (most often a mother or a sister) or a lesbian partner may share the responsibilities of child care. In general a single mother is more likely to face financial hardship as well as the stress of sole responsibility for one or more child.

Facing prejudice
Although some forms of single parenthood, for example widowhood, carry comparatively little stigma, any woman without a man may be perceived as having less status in a society which is still strongly dominated by patriarchal values. An increasing number of children are born to parents who are not married. However the residual prejudice against illegitimacy is likely to be felt most keenly by young unmarried single mothers and their children. Such mothers have become the latest easy target for politicians wishing to deflect blame for social ills, ranging from delinquency and housing shortages to the state of the economy, on to a heterogeneous group which is not in a position to answer the accusations. In right wing politics and journalism, the 'problem of single parent mothers' usually refers to the difficulties 'they' allegedly create rather than the problems many of them face.

"You're the only person who's ever said anything good about me as a mother"

Some single mothers not only miss the emotional support fathers are traditionally meant to provide, but also carry with them the legacy of a relationship in which they have been unappreciated and criticized. Sara and her two sons, Peter, aged four, and Steven, almost two, were refugees from Africa (see also Chapter 2) and had also escaped from the threat of violence from Sara's partner. They faced financial hardship and Sara had experienced racist attitudes from a number of the professionals she had encountered during the family's entry to Britain and in her efforts to obtain practical help for herself and her children. She was advised at a Child Health Clinic to seek therapy because both children seemed to be in an anxious state and Peter, the elder boy, had begun to have violent tantrums which Sara felt helpless to manage.

At their first appointment, both boys were extremely subdued. They sat close to their mother and did not venture from her side to explore the room or play with toys which had been laid out within easy reach. When their mother encouraged them to play, Peter appeared anxious and, as well as refusing to play himself, actively discouraged his brother from picking anything up. Frightened himself, his motivation for discouraging Steven appeared to be protective. Although Sara had come for help with her children she appeared to need to talk about the dangers, injustices and hardships which her family had faced. Her story was a moving one and the most appropriate solution focused questions that the therapist could ask were "How did you cope?" "How did you get through such a terrible ordeal?" "What made you determined to keep going?"

The atmosphere during feedback was sombre as the family's exceptionally stressful history was recognized. Sara's courage and self sacrifice on behalf of her children were acknowledged. Her determination in the face of bureaucracy was admired and her open-mindedness in agreeing to meeting with a therapist was complimented. The therapist noted Peter's apparently protective actions toward his younger brother.

After Sara and her sons left the first session, the team continued to feel overawed by the problems the family had faced and continued to face and decided that therapy was likely to play a small part in resolving them. In retrospect, it seems we were underestimating the resources of the family and the power of compliments. By the second session the children had 'unfrozen' sufficiently to play together in the room, and by the third the lighter mood of Sara and her sons made us suspect that they had been recipients of some unexpected good fortune, housing or perhaps some much needed financial assistance. This was not the case. Life had continued to be tough but Sara said she had learnt something that had given her some more hope. She paid the therapist a compliment when she said "You're the first person who ever said anything good about me as a mother" and made it clear that the therapist's words had helped her.

"What with my menopause and her adolescent mood swings…"

Absent fathers may be idealized or demonized by their children and ex-partners. Rachel, a white British woman in her late forties, and her daughter Emma, aged 16, both wanted help because they were worried and distressed by the escalating arguments which they had been having over the previous year. Rachel had separated from Emma's father when her daughter was still a baby and had a second child, Ashley, aged 12, by another man who travelled as part of his work and who had lived with the family "on and off" until Ashley was about three years old. Emma's father had maintained contact with her and, since he married about seven years ago, had been having Emma to stay with him and his new family each summer holiday. Ashley's father maintained infrequent and unpredictable contact with his son, usually in the form of brief visits and occasional presents.

My first impression of the family was of three articulate and outspoken individuals who showed a great deal of loyalty to one another and who were confused and unsettled by the rows between mother and daughter which had been happening several times a week. Rachel said she felt completely undermined by the rows and expressed her frustration that after years of "being mother and father" to Emma and Ashley she no longer felt she could cope. She attributed her clashes with Emma to the "raging hormones" which seemed to be driving both of them. At times Emma threatened to leave home and to go to live permanently with her father. Much as it distressed her, Rachel felt so defeated she could not come up with an alternative solution. She said she had anticipated that her daughter would leave home in a couple of years anyway and was beginning to think that Emma was right in saying her father could be a better parent to her until then.

Exploration of exceptions focused on the times Emma and Rachel were not being pushed around by their hormones. In this way I was using the technique of 'externalizing the problem', instigated by White[42]. They were then asked about the things each of them would miss about the other if Emma were to leave home. When Rachel and Emma ran out of examples, Ashley provided more. Despite telling his sister that he would not mind being deprived of her bossing him around, he also made it clear that he was usually glad to see Emma after her holiday visits to her father. He too would miss her if she moved permanently. A picture emerged of a mother and daughter who were each competent in their activities outside the home, Rachel in her career, Emma at school, who cooperated successfully in many household tasks and who were capable of debate as well as argument. Rachel said proudly that she had always encouraged her children to think for themselves.

Feedback to the family highlighted their mutual warmth and loyalty and acknowledged the hurt and confusion resulting from a problem which had seemed soluble only by separation. Their forthright style was complimented: "Rachel did a good job nurturing independent thinking. Now Emma is no longer a child but an adolescent, it is inevitable that that skill will sometimes be turned on her mother " Rachel was also congratulated for having raised her family in a way which challenged sex role stereotypes. For example, she was the family breadwinner and both daughter and son had been encouraged to be sensitive to emotional issues as well as to be able to stand up for themselves. In view of this, the therapist said she felt the "raging hormones" theory did not do justice to Rachel and Emma, especially as the evidence (in the form of exceptions) was overwhelmingly against such an explanation.

Emma and Rachel accepted that their rows might be seen as a normal stage in the development of their family and decided that they should try to sort out their conflicts without Emma leaving. The goals for the family became, firstly, to find ways to cope with ordinary conflicts between a young person and a parent and, secondly, to prepare everyone for the changes that would occur as Ashley entered adolescence and when Emma left home to go to college.

"A single parent with a psychiatric history"

Traditionally, mothers are expected to be more responsible for nurturing, fathers for discipline. Single mothers may feel less confident about discipline and may be seen as having less authority with their children, especially boys, than a father would. Jerome's school doctor saw his mother as likely to be ineffective because she was not only a single parent of a son but also someone with a psychiatric history. Sonia, an Afro-Caribbean single mother and her son Jerome, aged 5, were referred by a school doctor because Jerome had found it difficult to settle in school, where he was disruptive and defiant, and appeared to be difficult for his mother to manage. The doctor mentioned that Sonia had seemed "emotionally rather flat". Prior to their first appointment, Sonia had made a special visit to school (see Chapter 2) and had agreed, with Jerome's class teacher, some consistent sanctions for unacceptable behaviour. During the first interview, Jerome's verbal fluency and advanced vocabulary for his age were striking. At times he used this facility to be cheeky and rude to his mother. In contrast, his mother spoke rather slowly, pausing before answering questions. She seemed hurt and exasperated by his insults and at a loss to know what to do. Jerome appeared intensely embarrassed by Sonia's descriptions of the problems which had brought them to therapy.

Exploration of exceptions drew out some surprising resources of both mother and son. As well as having some good days at school, and being considered a child with a lot of potential by his class teacher, Jerome could almost always be relied upon to behave calmly and appropriately in church. Sonia had clearly had a strong influence in helping Jerome to learn how to behave in that setting and felt supported as a parent by members of the congregation. The activity he and his mother particularly enjoyed together in the evenings was playing the spelling board game, Scrabble. It also emerged that they shared a sense of humour and that laughter could transform Sonia's otherwise subdued expression.

When I next spoke to the referrer, he drew my attention to the fact that Sonia had a psychiatric history, implying that working with the family might be difficult for that reason. It seemed unfortunate that a psychiatric label, combined with Sonia's single parenthood might obscure her capabilities as a mother. I was happy to report that I had enjoyed meeting with the family, that Sonia had already taken the initiative to contact the school prior to seeing me, that she was making a contribution to her son's education and that we had identified some problem-free times on which to build.

Giving the next generation of men the chance to be different
In a climate of accusations that single parent families produce delinquent children, the label of failure, and all the self fulfiling prophecy which that entails, can be hard for a single mother to shift. Julia and her son Aaron, aged 13, of an Afro- Caribbean family, came back to a clinic at which they had received help in the past, at Julia's request. The records showed that when Aaron was 6 years old he had been on the Child Protection Register following a 'non-accidental injury' by his mother.

After a problem-free discussion that encompassed the subjects of the family's journey to the appointment, difficulty finding the building, and what Aaron and his mother would usually be doing at that time on a Wednesday afternoon, the conversation moved on to the purpose of their visit to a therapist. It emerged that Julia was currently worried about Aaron stealing, and especially angry that he had taken money from her purse. Sensing that inviting Julia to speak at length about the problem would lead to Aaron becoming more reticent and, realising that I knew very little about the family, I asked what changes had taken place since making the appointment.

Julia I've decided they have too much freedom, Aaron and his brother, so I've said they've got to cook the Sunday lunch.

Therapist That's you and your brother. Who is at home?

Aaron My Mum, my brother and my sister.

Therapist How old is your brother?

Aaron Eleven.

Therapist And your sister?

Aaron Two and a half.

Therapist So she can't help much with the Sunday lunch.

Aaron (laughs)

Therapist What sorts of things do you make for lunch?

Aaron Sometimes we take it in turns so that what he did last week I do this week and what I did last week he does this week, like one week he will cook the rice and peas and the potatoes and peel it and everything and I would cook the chicken and then next week we would swap over.

Therapist Right...do you do the preparation as well, d'you go to the shop?

Aaron No... we help my mum do the shopping sometimes, mostly some of it's already started for us but what's left we do that.

Therapist How do you and your brother decide who's going to do what each week? Can you decide quite peacefully or do you have a big argument about it? How do you decide?

Aaron Well, last week I'll have done the chicken and he'll have done the rest so this week we just swap over.

Therapist So it's pretty clear. Who was it understood who should do what the first time? Who decided?

Aaron (smiles) My mum did.

Therapist Ah right, she got the ball rolling. (to Julia) How was it you decided they were ready to take the responsibility?

Julia When they was little I taught them first how to make hot drink then after that toast and then eventually they wanted to fry an egg and I got them to that and then to use a grill. As they developed they could handle it and putting fast food in the oven that kind of thing - produce a brilliant meal from all the frozen stuff and I thought it was time to take it a stage further. I thought if I'm ever ill or if for their own personal benefit I think its useful for them to cook. I mean I've taught them to do house work, clean the whole house, ironing and all that aspect. At the end of the day it will be helpful to them. When I've finished with them they should be independent, they won't be forced in a relationship for their convenience.

Therapist So they won't just be looking for someone to do their ironing for them?

Julia (nods and laughs)

Therapist (laughs) I'm impressed because ironing is quite a responsibility. Did it take a lot of supervising?

Julia It took a lot of supervising, a lot of teaching, to iron the different kinds of material and grade the iron (laughs). When they get a couple of shirts ironed by mum it's a treat now.

Therapist ... it sound as though there have been a lot of changes around your home recently.

Julia Yes.

Aaron Yeah.

Therapist Any other changes for me to hear about?

Julia spoke of the action she had taken following her decision to put a stop to Aaron's stealing once and for all. She had stopped his pocket money, complained to some figures of authority in their local community and threatened to get him put into a boarding school if he did not shape up. It emerged that there had been no stealing over the previous two weeks but that she felt it was early days. When asked about her confidence in her son's ability to resist temptation to take money, she said she felt he was about half way to resisting completely. Aaron estimated his ability to resist at about 2 out of 10.

The following feedback was given at the end of the session:

Therapist First thing to say is how much I've enjoyed talking to you because you both have some really interesting ideas and you also have a very direct way of saying things, so I think you managed to catch me up with a lot in a very short time, and I appreciate that. (to Julia) I wouldn't like to embarrass your son by singing his praises too much but there are one or two things that I'd particularly like to mention. They're things that I noticed as someone who meets quite a lot of young people. I found him very polite, very frank in his answers, very thoughtful. (directly to Aaron) I think when you weren't quite sure what to say you gave it some time, gave it some thought and when it came the time to ask you about resisting temptation, I think you gave a very honest answer. You could have pretended you found it a lot easier but you rated yourself at 2 and a half, quite realistic, quite honest, quite modest about where you have got to, whereas (to Julia) as a mother I think you can see his potential a bit more so you, strangely enough, at this moment, you're a bit more confident...I think it must be pleasing for a mother to recognize... I just so admire your initiative in getting your boys doing things that will enable them to stand on their own feet and it even sounds like you've done it in a way that has enabled them to enjoy it because (to Aaron) Aaron, the way you talked made it sound as if you quite like making the dinner and that you and your brother get on together...this kind of practice sounds a really great idea and (to Julia) I also get the feeling that things have got to the stage where you think they should do a little more and you should do a little less (Julia smiles and nods).

(to Aaron) I think the only way you are going to get as much practice as you need is if your mum could leave out some little bits of money...resisting temptation needs practice and, just as your chicken will improve with practice, I guess resisting temptation could improve with practice as well. (to Julia) It's asking you to do a little bit more but I hope it won't be too arduous.

Julia Well, he knows the consequences so I'll do that for the ultimate goal... at the moment he's not getting any pocket money at all. He's got a couple of weeks out because of (paying back what he had taken), after that I will review. (to Aaron) You've got that time to prove to me you're worthy of getting that money back.

By the next appointment, there had been no further incidents of stealing and Aaron had received some pocket money. Julia said she would remain watchful for some time to come before she trusted him. Both mother and Aaron wanted to devote the session to discussing a difference of opinion common to many parents and teenagers, about staying out late and the young person's choice of friends.

As with many single mothers, it would be easy to tell Julia's story with an emphasis on failure. A solution focused approach enabled her to tell a different story, one which showed her skills as a mother, her thoughtful and practical approach to her sons' independence and her determination to tackle a current problem.

Single mothers generally have a 'bad Press'. They frequently blame themselves for any difficulties with their children while overlooking their achievements as parents. Solution Focused Brief Therapy provides a gentle but powerful challenge to this perspective.

Chapter 4
Children should be heard when seen

When first brought to see a therapist, often following referral by a professional who has accentuated the problems of one individual in the family, a child will often have the impression he or she is there because of being naughty. Children have frequently experienced criticism and blame from their parents and other siblings. Parents often feel at the end of their tether and may only be willing to meet a therapist when they have exhausted all other options available to them. Understandably they often arrive feeling defeated and frustrated. These are far from ideal circumstances in which to have your point of view heard, if you are a child who is 'the identified patient'. Solution Focused Brief Therapy offers a number of ways to open up fresh perspectives on families' situations for both children and parents and to give children an opportunity to participate actively in meetings with their therapist.

Lifting the 'problem child' label.
Problem-free talk and discussion of exceptions enable parents to recollect that their children are multi-faceted individuals and to describe them in ways which include accomplishments and lovable qualities. Such conversations encourage parents to recognize their own successful influence in aspects of their children's development which are going well. Parents are often pleasantly surprised to find themselves experiencing an unfamiliar or long forgotten sense of pride in their children. Children who have grown accustomed to a pattern, of criticism and entreaties to improve, are frequently relieved and pleased to hear their parents' words of appreciation. The lifting of blame from 'problem' children early in the first conversation with the therapist frequently liberates them to take part, encouraging the voicing of their opinions and incorporation of their point of view into the description of exceptions and goals.

Understandable language
Concrete descriptions are a feature of all solution focused conversations, whether with adults or children. This enables children to follow

the discussion between adults as easily as possible and facilitates their involvement. The therapist seeks to obtain clear and concrete descriptions of any abstract concepts. This approach is particularly valuable to children when the therapist is trying to reach a common understanding of concepts like "showing more respect", "behaving" or "acting your age", which often mean more to adults than to children.

Children generally find questions beginning with "why" impossible to answer. Parents have often made frustrating attempts to uncover their childrens' 'reasons' for certain behaviour by asking, for example:

"Why do you wet the bed?"

"Why don't you concentrate more at school?"

"Why can't you be nicer to your sister?"

"Why must you be so aggressive with other children?"

Solution focused therapists avoid "why" questions. They listen to family members' own hypotheses about problems and often address the issue of motivation or explanation for problems in their feedback to clients toward the end of a session. However, they concentrate on asking questions which begin "how?", "when?", "where?", "which?", "what?" and "what else?" These are questions designed to draw out clear recognizable descriptions of exceptions and wished for improvements. For example:

"When was the last time you managed not to wet the bed?"

"What would you see him doing in class when he begins concentrating better?"

"When is she is nicer to her sister? What does she do with her at those times?"

"What do you do with other children that your parents are pleased about?....What else?"

Utilizing children's imagination

An approach which includes 'miracles' and rating scales offers an adaptable framework for child and family work. The miracle question may be explained to children in terms of magic or wishes and fits well with their view of the world and the prospects opened up by imagination. Rating scales can be represented pictorially, as stepping stones across a river, steps on a ladder, or the distance from the bottom to the top of a hill. etc.

"Do something different"

However troubled children may be, they are not usually the members of the family who decide to seek, or to take up, help. Adults who are responsible for them do so. However powerful children may seem, for example when keeping the household up all night or making a major public scene in the supermarket, their relative influence within families reflects their lack of the kinds of power associated with the greater knowledge, strength, and status which adults possess. It is difficult, although not always impossible, for a child to take the initiative in setting chosen changes in motion.

Parents frequently ask therapists for advice about ways of managing what they perceive as problem behaviour on the part of children. The advice received from solution focused therapists tends to be a variation on the theme of "If it works, do more of it" and "If it's not working, do something different". Opinions differ among such therapists about how much attention should be paid to parental approaches which are not being effective, especially when they include smacking. Since a parent once asked me "He doesn't stop it when I smack him, do you think I should try smacking him harder next time?", I have favoured exploring the subject in some detail and trying to find out whether it is something the parent would prefer to give up. Usually it is. Provided no information necessitating concerns about child protection emerges, I usually end by saying that, for a variety of reasons, including the pragmatic, I would recommend giving up smacking and putting energy into other approaches.

Child-friendly goals

It is a principle of solution focused work that goals should be selected by the client(s). Kelley's mother, Kathy, wanted her thirteen year daughter to get to school on time, behave better in class and stop getting detentions. Kelley's main interest at school was spending time with her friends and irritating Ms. Wright, the teacher she most disliked. She complained that she was often blamed for things she had not done, as well as those she had, and wanted to be "picked on" less. It appeared that her dislike of Ms. Wright was not without some justification. The teacher appeared to have made a self-fulfiling prophecy about Kelley being from a bad family and therefore bound to be bad in school.

The therapist discussed with mother and daughter the possibility that each could achieve what she wanted; the event most likely to irritate and upset Ms. Wright would be to be proved wrong in her estimation of Kelley's potential. Thus both mother's and daughter's objectives would be fulfiled by Kelley suddenly behaving more acceptably in school. Kelley seemed interested in the idea but said that even if her behaviour improved, as she was confident it could, her teacher would not notice. Ms. Wright had never acknowledged her comparatively good conduct in art lessons. We then discussed how much improvement would be required to give Ms. Wright a shock and shake her conviction that Kelley was a bad pupil, even if she might try to hide her surprise. The idea appealed to Kelley's sense of humour. She suddenly saw the possibility of defying Ms. Wright without getting herself into trouble. She eventually managed, to her great satisfaction, to provoke a flicker of astonishment from her teacher.

"For responsibility, I'd give him 10 out of 10"

Alex, aged 14, and his mother, Maria, had attended two appointments because of her concerns about what she felt was underachievement at school, lack of effort with homework and excessive shyness. Alex's parents were of white European background. Both mother and son were dissatisfied with the pattern of "nagging" (Maria's own word) and procrastination that had developed between them at home. There had been a slight improvement in homework output since mother relaxed a little and spoke of homework less.

An assessment of Alex's abilities showed that he was generally within the average range for his age but that he had a greater facility for practical tasks than for verbal ones. It was clear that if his written work were to improve, it would require extra effort on his part as well as more guidance from school. Part of Maria's miracle was that Alex's father, Nicholas, become more involved with his son's education. A special invitation was extended for the next session, as Alex's father had not yet joined any of the meetings. He attended the next meeting, at which it emerged that he was also concerned about Alex's progress and had experienced some similar problems himself at school. He too had had a good understanding of practical classes but had found it difficult to put ideas down on paper. He also shared Maria's view about their son's quietness and had taken some steps to try to help. He explained that he had begun to encourage some age-appropriate activities out of school as well as inviting Alex to accompany him to work, in his own small business, sometimes at weekends.

Alex's father gave the impression of seeing less to complain about. His son, however, remained quiet and subdued throughout the first half of the conversation. He appeared to expect each question to be followed by a critical comment, until the therapist began to elicit ratings from Alex and his parents. All rated an improvement in Alex's attitude to school work, completion of homework and signs that he was taking steps toward more contact with his peers. Father extended the use of the scale by suddenly remarking that he would award him 10 out of 10 for responsibility when visiting his workplace. He said that his son deserved a rating of 9 or 10 for most other aspects of behaviour. He thought Alex compared favourably with many of their friends' children as well as with many of Alex's classmates. Alex looked first astonished then almost unrecognizably pleased. His mother readily agreed with her husband's praise of Alex's conduct.

The session marked a turning point in Alex's confidence. His father's creative use of the rating scale opened up a channel of communication, about success and approval, within the family. It challenged the problem-dominated story with which Alex had arrived in therapy. The family left that meeting with Alex appearing proud of himself after his parents had shown their appreciation of his many admirable qualities. There was less chance that he and his mother would repeat the nagging and procrastination cycle of which both were weary. If Alex took even a little of his new-found confidence into social situations with his peers they would be likely to find him more approachable.

Lightening the burden of the past

At first sight, it may be daunting to maintain a solution focus with a client who continues to suffer, following severe early losses or abuses. What can one say to a child whose miracle would be that a parent was alive again or that they had never been abused or rejected? In such cases it may be tempting to move away from Solution Focused Brief Therapy toward other approaches; there are, after all, many prescriptions for long term therapeutic programmes.

The part of West London in which I work is ethnically and cultur-
ally very mixed. It includes refugees and families or parts of families
who have come to Britain in an attempt to escape extreme financial
hardship. Sometimes children have been uprooted from everything and
everyone they know to join relatives here. I have worked with a number of families like this, from Morocco and other parts of Africa and
from the Caribbean.

Michael was ten years old when I first met him, together with his
father, Lawrence. Michael had been described by the referring school
doctor as "suicidally depressed" and she suggested that the solution to
his problems, which also included getting into fights at school, making
poor academic progress and being disruptive in class, would be to
"send him home to his mother".

Michael's parents, both of African origin, had separated when he
was two years old. Lawrence had come to Britain while Michael
remained with his mother, living in comparative poverty, until the age
of ten when one of his father's relatives had gone to collect him, to
bring him to join his father. This process was viewed as rescue from
hardship by Michael's father's side of the family. It was not possible to
elicit his mother's view. From Michael's point of view, she had let him
go and had done little to keep in touch, despite attempts to reach her
by letter and to send messages with other family members.

At first I wondered whether father might agree with the doctor, that
his son should be sent "home" but he was adamant that the boy should
stay, that it was his duty as a father to raise him and that he would
work hard to help Michael to cope in an unfamiliar family, school,
country and culture. Lawrence's efforts were to include attending
meetings with Michael's teachers, participating in therapy, and educating the professionals involved about his culture's customs, especially the courtesies expected between adults and children in families. At
that first meeting, Michael said little, looking the way that had
prompted the doctor's description of him.

As a psychologist I was involved both in offering therapy and con-
tributing to describing Michael's educational needs. In retrospect, I see
that I allowed a number of the assumptions I then held about loss to
guide my work with the family, rather than trusting to their own capacities to cope with and find solutions to their difficulties. I have since

read a number of helpful articles on the subject, to which I refer below, which contribute to this perspective, with hindsight, on my work with Michael and his family.

Through a mixture of family sessions, for Michael, his father and occasionally his grandmother, individual sessions for Michael, and liaison with Michael's teachers, some goals were negotiated. Michael and his father still appeared like strangers to one another, a fact which distressed them both and led to many misunderstandings. The first goal was that Michael and Dad should get on better. Lawrence spelt out various expectations concerning Michael's participation in chores at home, the need to tell his father where he was going when playing out and to come home at the agreed time. He wanted his son to work hard at learning to read and write and to reject bad company (mainly involvement with children who engaged in illegal activities like shoplifting). In turn he agreed to teach him the skills needed at home, including some cooking, and to spend time showing Michael London. Michael wanted regular opportunities to spend time with his cousins and to have his father's company listening to music or watching television in the evening. As mutual wishes and expectations became clearer, father and son ceased to appear strangers to one another and a sense of cooperation developed between them, with occasional arguments and renegotiations.

The second set of objectives concerned education and can be summarized as Michael doing better and being happier in school. It seemed that this could only be achieved by Michael being able to understand lessons better, by learning to control his temper and by making some friends in class. Michael changed school to one with smaller classes and additional individual teaching. It was agreed that Michael would receive help with the lessons he had previously found difficult, and that he could speak to his teacher or leave the room to "cool off" at times when he felt upset or angry, for example when his classmates teased him about his mother. Unfortunately comments about mothers are one of the most frequent taunts used in any teasing by school children and Michael was highly sensitive to such remarks. If he did lose his temper or behave aggressively toward other children, he was to be subject to the usual school discipline. After a stormy term, Michael developed a trusting relationship with his teacher. He began to be able to anticipate better when he felt himself getting agitated and was more often able to calm down on his own or by talking with his teacher. He became one of the more popular pupils with his classmates and started to concentrate more on his work, even though he continued to find it difficult.

Thirdly, and perhaps most importantly for Michael, was the goal of coping with missing his mother and half siblings. I spent some of the individual sessions with Michael finding out what his life in Africa had been like. I searched for clues to the best way to facilitate his coping with what I deduced, from the emotions he conveyed nonverbally, to be a mixture of confusion, misery and anger. His father and grandmother helped him to to try to contact his mother by letter and through relatives but there was no reply to Michael and meagre information. The family sessions acknowledged the past but focused on the present and future. The individual sessions were devoted to making a book of photos, drawings and writings by Michael about his earlier life. He said little about his family in Africa and I found it difficult to draw him out.

From time to time I arranged review appointments with Michael and his father and/or the school. Despite great progress in terms of the warmth and cooperation between father and son and growing success in school, the stress of loss appeared to hang heavily on Michael. I was unsure whether I was helping any progress to be made in enabling him to cope with the burden. No doubt sensing my good intentions but slow or non-existent progress, Michael's father said he would like his son to be able to come to see me until he was an adult.

I realise now that I had taken on the impossible task of helping Michael to say "goodbye" to his mother. I had overlooked the ways in which Michael and his father were themselves dealing with the feelings aroused by the separation. Unfortunately at that stage I had not read White's inspiring paper[43] about "saying hullo" to those grieved for, and had, I think, been working in accord with my own assumptions about Michael's grief. I had been assuming that his loss was final and total. I was to discover that my assumptions were out of step with Michael's experience.

I carried out the next, and what turned out to be the final, review in a rigorously solution focused way, gauging progress and room for improvement in relation to each of the goals. When we came to discussing the burdens of the past separation it was clear there was still some way to go. I asked Michael what had helped him to cope, so far, and he replied that he looked ahead to the time when, as an adult, he would be able to go to Africa and visit his Mum. For the time being, speaking with Dad about these plans, about his Mum and about Africa helped him to cope with his feelings. At that session both they and I recognised that they no longer needed any assistance from me. A follow up after six months showed that things were going well.

White has challenged the prevailing assumption about bereavement and separation, that they are essentially processes culminating in letting go or "saying goodbye" to the person lost and fully accepting the permanence of their loss. He believes the metaphor of "saying hullo" can be helpful. He encourages therapists to facilitate the process of clients, who have experienced bereavement, separation or rejection, developing their treasured memories of the person whom they have lost. He argues that some effects of loss are undeniably permanent, for example the physical company of the person who has gone and once shared plans for the future. However there are other ways in which clients' experiences of lost loved ones can be present. He often asks clients to imagine themselves through the eyes of the person who is no longer with them.

There is no solution to bereavement and many other forms of loss. They are an unwelcome but inevitable and natural part of life. For many the process of recovery, although painful and exhausting, is natural and straightforward. In such cases there is little, if any, role for therapy or counselling. Other individuals find the process of gradual recovery eluding them and experience life being dominated by their loss in a way which feels endless and hopeless. Solutions can be found to coping with the effects of loss. There is no reason to deprive clients, who are preoccupied with or burdened by the past, of solution focused approaches.

From fighting together to singing together

Theresa, aged 7, Anna, aged 4 and their mother, Elisa, were from a family of mixed race and Latin American origin. They came to see a therapist because Elisa felt she could no longer cope with Theresa's tantrums, defiance, verbal abuse and "spiteful" behaviour toward her sister. She was also worried because her elder daughter seemed unhappy most of the time and appeared to be reluctant to go to school. She explained that she was much more concerned about Theresa than her husband because she spent more time with the children and that he had not wished to accompany them to see a therapist for help. Although I asked some questions, throughout all the sessions with Elisa and her daughters, about changes father might be expected to notice as their problems resolved, I did not attempt to convene meetings of the whole family. It seemed likely from the end of the first session that working with those who attended that meeting would be likely to facilitate the changes both mother and Theresa wanted.

It was difficult to devote much time in the first meeting to problem-free talk because mother clearly wanted to express her grievances about Theresa. Elisa said she felt Theresa had always resented Anna and that her behaviour had gone downhill to the point where mother and daughter were constantly in conflict. When not expressing intense anger with her elder daughter, she voiced her concern about Theresa's evident unhappiness. Theresa sat sulking during her mother's outpouring of frustration and anxiety. Each of the girls responded to questions addressed directly to them but gave the impression of being eager to keep a low profile while the adults had a serious talk. Anna began playing with a doll's house and Theresa joined her. Out of the corner of my eye I could see that there were occasional opportunities for squabbles between the two sisters. These disagreements somehow came to nothing, without any adult intervention being required.

I asked Elisa about exceptions and her miracle, a concept which she initially appeared to find ridiculous, then amusing, then thought provoking. She said she would know at once if a miracle happened. Theresa would smile and say "good morning" and then cooperate in washing and dressing herself. Theresa would not cry before school and would be in a good mood. She went on to describe a harmonious day. Elisa said that she herself would be different too, more patient, less tempted to smack, smiling more and praising Theresa sometimes. She said she wanted both girls to have a better childhood than she had been given and that she felt that she had often failed to fulfil that wish, revealing the extent to which she blamed herself for difficulties with Theresa.

Theresa stopped playing and listened attentively. It emerged that Elisa had seen tantalizing glimpses of her miracle already. When asked to give a rating, of the present situation, on a scale from 0 (worst ever) to 10 (after the miracle), Elisa replied "two to three". I turned to Theresa who seemed more ready to participate than she had earlier and said that her mother seemed to be saying that things had been worse, with more arguments at home and more unhappiness, but had got a little better. I said I thought Mummy wanted them to get even better, like the miracle she had described. I asked Theresa whether she wanted things to get better too. When she nodded her head vigorously, I drew a hill for her on a piece of paper, explaining that at the bottom of the hill were all the problems and up at the top it was like her miracle. I invited her to draw something at the top of the hill which she thought would be a good thing to have in a problem free happy place. She drew a stick figure with a happy face. At the bottom of the hill she drew a figure with a down turned mouth. When I asked her to draw a picture of a person to indicate where she felt she was on the path up the hill to her personal miracle, she chose a point about a quarter of the way from the bottom of the hill. Thus she indicated that she wished for just as much improvement as her mother did, even though at that point it was not possible to elucidate the details of her miracle.

The atmosphere had lightened considerably during discussion of the miracle and rating scales. Elisa was clearly surprised to learn that Theresa also thought there were problems which she was hoped to see resolved. Feedback at the end of the session included: affirming Elisa's aspirations for her family, noting Theresa and Anna's capacity to play and show warmth to one another, despite the evident pain of sibling rivalry, and commending Theresa's willingness to explain things to the therapist in pictures. Theresa and her mother looked startled and pleased by the compliments. The therapist encouraged them to notice the things that each of them did that helped glimpses of their miracles to occur.

The cycle of complaints by Elisa, and sulks and defiance by Theresa, began to change in the first session, which appeared to engender some hope for mother and daughter. There was gradual progress over three subsequent sessions in which I heard of the improvements in interaction between mother and Theresa at home. I learned that Theresa had started to talk to her mother about her reasons for being unhappy about school, thereby enabling Elisa to help. Elisa's ratings and Theresa's drawings showed that each felt close to her miracle. Elisa explained that she was teaching Theresa and Anna some songs from her own country of origin, something she wanted to share with both of them, and that the three of them had great fun singing together. Having come to therapy to find a way out of conflict, the special shared warmth of singing together seemed a bonus.

Solution Focused Brief Therapy has some built-in advantages for children. It facilitates the development of a comfortable atmosphere in which strengths rather than deficiencies are highlighted. Conversation between all participants in therapy, whether children or adults, emphasizes concrete descriptions which children can grasp and utilizes imagination in ways which are commonplace to children. Having fostered an atmosphere in which it feels safe to join in, children are then given the opportunity to participate and to communicate their goals for therapy.

Chapter 5
Safe remembering

Over the past ten to twenty years the prevalence and long term effects of child sexual abuse have been recognized. A growth area for techniques of diagnosis and new orthodoxies of therapy has developed, many emphasizing what appears to me to be an almost confrontational approach. Those therapists using psychodynamic approaches have stressed the need for clients to revisit abusive experiences in detail in the company of a therapist who can assist them to express their feelings[44]. Therapists influenced by feminism have paid attention to the gender of the therapist and have in some cases argued that, in general, male therapists should not see clients who have been abused by men[45]. A number of brief therapists, including Yvonne Dolan[23], Bill O'Hanlon[46], Kate Kowalski[47] and Michael Durrant[48] have challenged these orthodoxies and demonstrated the flexibility of working in a solution focused or solution oriented way with victims of child sexual abuse and other traumas, including rape.

Durrant writes of the 'out-of-controlness' that many children who have been sexually abused, or otherwise ill treated, continue to experience. They have been the victims of activities over which they had no real control. He points out that many of the approaches designed to let children 'talk through' their experiences or 'work through' their feelings may inadvertently heighten their sense of still being out of control. He favours an approach in which the adverse influence of past experiences may be externalized so that the child can be invited to 'stand up to the Past' or to receive help to 'stop being pushed around by the Past'. In this way children can begin to feel a greater sense of control over memories and over present behaviour.

Dolan employs solution focused ideas and Ericksonian hypnotic techniques in creative and original ways. She offers a number of helpful insights into the experiences of those who have been sexually abused. She believes that some of the symptoms, especially dissociation under stress, suffered by adults who were sexually abused as children, were strategies for survival in childhood which have outlived their usefulness. Dolan cautions therapists about the possibility of reabusing clients by insensitive questioning about the past. While recognizing that talking about the abuse has the potential to be helpful, she feels that clients should have control over their own stories, especially over the pace and extent of disclosure in therapy.

She points out that clients may need to reach a stable point in their lives, sometimes by resolving other problems, before tackling the memories of abuse. In the case of clients who are children, they may need help putting a boundary around a trauma to deal with later when they are developmentally able. Children are at special risk of becoming retraumatised by the evocation of memories they cannot understand. Dolan uses drawing with child clients who are invited to draw the trauma, then to draw the exception or imagined exception or resolution to the trauma and finally to make a picture showing the process of getting from the trauma to the resolution, in other words "Draw how things got from bad to O.K."

Symbols of safety and resourcefulness

In Dolan's view, the therapist should take a protective stance toward the client. Early in the contact with clients, techniques are taught to enable them to experience some sense of control over the pace of remembering and to enable symptom relief while treatment continues. Clients are helped to identify symbols of safety and well-being and to make use of them as anchors during turbulent emotional times during and between therapeutic sessions. For example, the clients write a 'rainy day letter' to themselves when feeling strong and hopeful, to remind themselves of their strengths and reasons for living. The letter can be read at times of stress, doubt or depression. Some clients prefer to make a tape. The 'medicine bundle' serves a similar function, of 'externalizing the solution'. Derived from the medicine rituals of the Native American culture, it comprises objects which symbolize the client's healing resources, for example, photographs of trusted figures, mementos of places associated with safety, something to symbolize strength, etc.

The letter or the bundle may be carried around or left in a place associated with stress where it can be helpful when needed. For instance a woman who used to cut herself "because it was the only way to feel real" was encouraged to leave her letter in the knife drawer to provide an alternative resolution to feelings of distress and detachment. Self-hypnotic relaxation is taught to allow the client the option of a soothing daydream at times of distress, for example during flash backs between sessions, or to slow the pace of remembering in therapy.

"Is that helpful to you?"
Nicky, a white British 17 year old had been beaten and sexually molested by a gang of young men. Six months later she continued to be troubled by flashbacks of vivid scenes from the assault, preoccupied by what had happened to her and distressed by her feelings of anger, defilement and guilt. On one occasion she had cut herself with a pair of scissors when unable to find any other way to get the flashbacks out of her mind. She sought help because she was afraid of harming herself again. She had also been finding it difficult to go out since the attack and was worried that she might become agoraphobic.

She was accompanied to her first appointment by her mother but said that she would prefer to speak with me on her own. After learning a little about Nicky's home, school activities and work ambitions, I explained to her that I wanted our talk to be helpful for her. I said that I was willing to listen to anything she wanted to tell me or that she thought it would help her to tell me, but that I did not wish her to feel under pressure to say more than that. I encouraged her to tell me if I asked her any question which she did not want to answer.

When asking her about the ways she had coped since the attack, it emerged that she had found some ways to help herself, for example talking to an aunt whom she trusted. She had also found other activities which made her feel worse. She described her evening routine which involved going to her room on her own and listening to melancholy music. She usually became miserable and preoccupied with self blame for the abuse she had endured. Flashbacks and disturbed nights often followed.

The principle "If something works, do more of it; if something isn't working, do something different" applies as much to recovery from trauma as to any other attempt at finding a solution to a difficulty. I said that I felt she had been very wise in finding someone she could trust, to talk to, and that her aunt appeared able to comfort her. She replied that her aunt had offered to see her at any time Nicky needed her, which appeared likely to be helpful in the future too. I then asked Nicky whether she thought solitude and mournful music was helping her. "I suppose not", she said, appearing surprised at the idea she might choose some other way to spend her evenings. It emerged that since the attack she had ceased a number of enjoyable evening activities, including helping her younger sister with her homework, watching television with her family and doing craft projects in her room.

I fed back to Nicky that I felt she had demonstrated to herself that the best situation in which to set aside time to think about the attack was in the company of her aunt. I suggested that she give up her current evening routine in favour of some of the activities she used to enjoy. Recognizing that she would still be likely to experience flashbacks and disturbed sleep, I taught her a self hypnotic technique, involving relaxation and imagery of a tranquil scene, for her to employ as "first aid" at times of distress.

She used subsequent sessions to tell me about the attack in the way she felt was helpful to her recovery. We were able to discuss her feelings and examine the guilt which many survivors of sexually abusive experiences feel. She continued to find comfort in the company of her aunt and through telling some close friends about what had happened to her. Her comment about the "first aid" strategy interested me. She explained that she had hardly needed to use it but that knowing it was available made her feel prepared for distress and less out of control.

Half way to recovery

Survivors of child sexual abuse have generally coped with the stress of being abused in ways which have a high emotional cost, for example by dissociating, keeping secret what was happening to them, self blame and self sacrifice. Adults, especially the abuser, may have depended upon these coping strategies being well developed. Survivors of abuse usually have a tried and tested capacity to "grin and bear it". Thus the questions a solution focused therapist should pose are not only "How did you cope?" and "How are you coping?" but also "Are you happy with this way of coping?" and "How would you like to see yourself coping?"

As with other problems, clients who seek help with the long term effects of child sexual abuse have often done a great deal to help themselves prior to seeing a therapist. Angie, a white British woman in her early twenties, was referred by her family doctor for help with anxiety and depressed mood thought to be associated with sexual abuse in childhood (See also Chapter 2). During the session it emerged that Angie felt half way to her miracle of recovery from abuse which would include losing the feeling of being dirty which had haunted her since childhood and being able to enjoy a sexual relationship with a man without being troubled by memories of the abuse. At the end of the session, the therapist gave the following feedback.

Therapist First of all, in a personal way, I feel very moved by what you have said about your experiences. As another woman I have been hearing about someone who has been subjected to the extreme end of the spectrum of abuse that men can bring to bear on women (and children).

Angie (Nods) Yes

Therapist The way you have described what that has meant to you has been very moving. I think you have been very courageous to come and talk about it...and I admire that very much indeed. It is part of what I see as enormous strengths and it would be quite easy for me to feel overawed by all you have managed to achieve for yourself. To have got half way to the kind of peace and self-respect you are looking for, by your own efforts is an amazing achievement. You have also made vivid to me the areas in which you think things could be better, in which you are not satisfied and in which you have further ambitions. I think those ambitions are justified...there are a number of clues in the things you have said about the kind of person you feel you are... You have done a number of things that have worked for you, including taking steps that other women who have been sexually abused often find helpful...you have spoken to your mother, you are exercising choice in your current relationship, you have found active ways to help life feel under your control and to demonstrate your care for yourself...you have found growing self-respect. You have done an enormous amount to admire and have an enormous amount of achievement to build on

Angie said that our conversation had helped her to realise how far she had ~lready come, how much she had done for herself and that she could probably do more. She decided not to arrange another appointment unless she felt the need for one in the future. In the light of the changes she had made which appeared to be in line with her wishes and to be good for her, I understood her decision not to make further appointments as a sign of self-confidence.

Vicarious learning about being blameless

The initiative shown by a white Irish woman, named Jacquie, in her early twenties, illustrates Dolan's view that clients are sometimes ready to cope with facing up to child sexual abuse once they have solved enough other difficulties to make life feel sufficiently stable. Jacquie saw a therapist at infrequent intervals over about 18 months to work on problems with work and certain family relationships. As she reached her goals, she explained that she had another problem which she wanted to talk about. The recent news that a friend had tried to kill himself had made her even more determined to get her own life in order. His action had reminded her of times in the past when she had been depressed and, with a sense of "there but for the grace of God go I", she felt she wanted to find a different way to cope.

Therapist...You spoke of your own feelings of depression and the ways you have found to cope with that...Say Ryan (the friend who attempted suicide) wants some advice, what would you say to him, from your experience?

Jacquie I just said to him "Don't let things get that bad that you want to kill yourself, it's just not worth giving up your life for, you know,...Don't let people get you down to the extent of giving up your own life".

Therapist So, what's the way of not letting things get on top of you that you used? Because you've had plenty of people who could have got on top of you...

Jacquie (I have) much more pride and stubbornness, I suppose....I think in my head, "They're not going to win."

Therapist So a bit of fighting talk helps

Jacquie ...I didn't really want to come here today, not because I didn't want to talk to you, but because there's something I want to say and it's so difficult. I've wanted to tell you so many times and I keep saying to myself, I'm going to tell you and I just couldn't tell you, and what it is is that when I was little I was abused, not by my dad, by a friend (of the family), it's so hard telling you now. Seeing Ryan this week...I just thought if I don't tell you today, I never would! I just can't believe I told you.

Therapist I think it's one of the hardest things to tell anyone.

Jacquie I'm shaking.

Therapist Mmm, but you decided to use your time and get on with saying that difficult thing.

Jacquie ... no one knows really, well my cousin knows and my sister and the reason it's all come out is I found out it happened to my sister Cathy as well. Oh God... my sister said "He tried to do things to me and all" and I felt so mad I felt worse that he had done it to her than to me. It sounds really strange, he made me so mad that he hurt her. I never thought I'd be able to tell you, I felt so terrible for so many years not telling anyone for so many years and I know the effect it has on people. Other girls I know, they all turned out crazy, one girl she'd try to kill herself...and another girl's a drug addict and I just don't want to be like that...I thought it's time I told you.

Therapist It's very frightening to think of how that pressure can affect people, but you haven't done any of those things. You haven't gone mad and you haven't turned to drugs. You've been trying to cope in different ways and now you've managed to talk about it too... I think most people find it's best to choose their time rather than be forced into it or say before they want to, so I think you've done the right thing.

Jacquie I know what happens to people, I've read so many things about it and watched so many programmes about it and I know people blame themselves and I do to an extent but I also feel angry now. I feel even more angry for what he did to my sister, I just feel like killing him... I suppose it's good in a way that I feel that angry.

Therapist (nods) You know he's the one who has done something wrong. What difference has it made talking to your sister?

Jacquie I suppose it was good but I was so shocked I didn't know it was happening to her. I didn't have a clue. I just feel angry and I feel angry with mum and dad they just kept sending me there.

Therapist ...and none of you had any choice because you were children.

Jacquie I didn't feel that until lately, until a while ago I used to think it was something I did wrong. I know it isn't really but the effect it has on you, it's just so strange, I don't trust people and a lot of it's (because of) that.

Therapist What's helped you come round to being very clear about whose fault it was?

Jacquie I don't know. Sorting out the other things in my life and really I'd read loads about it and seeing the other girls and being able to say so clearly it wasn't their fault, but when it came to me, I blamed myself, and then for a long time I tried not to think about it. I didn't remember it. I don't know for how many years I forgot... I know that sounds mad but I just blanked it out of my head.

Therapist And is that something you've read about being a very natural thing?

Jacquie Yeah, I have read that that's happened and after I remembered I thought "How did you blank that out?" but I just did, I didn't consciously do it. I just did it.

Therapist Of the talking and the reading that you've done, what have you found helpful for yourself?

Jacquie I don't know really that you can - not get over it- but not feel guilty - there's another way forward, just telling you. Telling people is one of the best thing ever because then it's not a secret and it has been a secret for so long. I didn't tell my cousin until I was about 16...I can't even believe I told you today.

Therapist So, being able to tell.

Jacquie That helps.

Therapist Being able not to blame yourself...you obviously know a lot about it from what you've read and talking to other people and thinking about yourself. What else has helped?

Jacquie I can't really think. I suppose the main thing that's in my head is it wasn't my fault, it wasn't my sister's fault. The only thing I can think now is I just want to tell you about it and I want to get it out of my system and get over it. I just don't want to be a victim any more. Can't even believe I had the courage to tell you today.

Therapist I think courage is the right word. I think you have a lot of it and this is one of the ways you've shown it.

Jacquie I feel so angry which is good because for so long I just kept putting it the back of my head but it's always there.

Therapist Anger has stood you in good stead in other situations and helped you to stand up for yourself. What has helped you get angry with this man?

Jacquie I suppose realising it wasn't my fault, it wasn't anything I did. I was a kid. It's only been recently (I realised)... I didn't even know what he was doing....

Jacquie's experience shows the value of exposing a secret by which she had felt trapped. Removing self blame is often an important part of recovery which in Jacquie's case was achieved by thinking about other victims of abuse and recognizing that they were not to blame. In an indirect way, she learnt that she too was not to blame.

Child sexual abuse is a trauma which can have long-lasting effects upon individuals. Much attention has been paid to the symptoms which are common to many victims or survivors of abuse and to their risk of becoming abusers or complicit in the abuse of children themselves. Less attention has been given to the ways in which some have found to cope and to avoid participating in an abused/abuser cycle. Solution Focused Brief Therapy is concerned with these important exceptions. The style of solution focused approach advocated by Dolan acknowledges the trauma, recognizes that victims may have developed some ways of coping which they may prefer to give up, offers 'first aid' techniques to give clients some control over symptoms and utilizes each client's unique contribution to their own recovery.

Chapter 6
Violence in the home

Like child sexual abuse, violence in the home, usually by a man toward a woman, is another family 'secret' that has been exposed in the last couple of decades. Working with clients who have been violent or who have been on the receiving end of violence presents the therapist with a number of moral dilemmas. Will a woman experience more violence as a result of what she says in therapy if the couple is seen together? How can the therapist offer therapy to women, who are frightened of further violence, and men, who are defensive about their previous violent acts? Does giving perpetrators of violence a respectful hearing, especially when the therapist is male, imply collusion?

The goal of non-violence
There are special difficulties facing a solution focused therapist. The situation is one in which it is not possible for the therapist to be neutral about goals, as is usually the practice; therapy can only remain ethical if one of its goals is that violence cease. There is an additional difficulty in identifying the usual small steps to the goal of non-violence, because preceding by gradual steps in degree or frequency of violence would be unacceptable.

The contribution of feminism
Violence between couples has been another fruitful area for the development of new orthodoxies, for example, that perpetrators must be treated in groups, that therapists should not see couples together when there has been violence, that couples must agree to live apart in order to be offered therapy, etc[49]. The topic of male on female violence in the home has prompted a feminist critique of the neutral interactional view of activities within relationships favoured by systemic family therapists. Virginia Goldner has made an important contribution to the debate[50], by highlighting the need to recognize the power imbalance involved in 'domestic violence' and the need to apportion responsibility to men for their violent actions. However, like Eve

Lipchik[49], she has challenged the use of specialized therapeutic programmes which require separation of partners. Together with her colleague, Gillian Walker, she offers therapy to some couples. They recognize the strong emotional bond, often compounded with financial dependency, that can exist in such relationships. Their approach respects the wishes of women who wish to stay with partners who have been violent to them, rather than implicitly criticizing or blaming them as approaches, which actively seek to influence women to leave, do.

Male responsibility to resist the urge to violence
Within the field of therapies concerned with solutions, both Alan Jenkins[51] and Bill O'Hanlon[52] have practical suggestions for working with men who have been violent. Jenkin extends to his clients an 'invitation to responsibility'. The therapist gently challenges a perpetrator's attributions of external causes for his violence, for example "What has stopped you from taking responsibility for your violence?". Further leading questions encourage the man to admit to his own culpability, to recognize the adverse effects of past actions on others and to begin to argue the case for a non-violent future. Thus therapist and client lay the foundations of a goal-directed method which emphasizes enabling the client to experience anger without responding violently. O'Hanlon also stresses the importance of breaking the link between feelings or fantasies and actions. He argues that the therapist should show an attitude of acceptance to any feelings or fantasies, however distasteful or violent they may appear. However, the therapist should make it clear that acting out violent fantasies is unacceptable and, furthermore, not inevitable. Thus the emphasis of the approach is on helping the client to resist the temptation to act, rather than to attempt the probably impossible task of stamping out feelings or fantasies.

A double perspective
Influenced by the writers cited above, we have found, in our work with couples, the need to emphasize both the need for control of violence by the man and for improving the chances of safety by the woman. While acknowledging that a perpetrator should be held accountable for his violent actions, we encourage women to take responsibility for doing all that is in their power to improve their safety. For example, for one

women this might involve arranging for another adult to be present at times at home, for another developing a contingency plan to enable her to leave, if necessary, for another taking legal steps to get an injunction to forbid her ex-partner to come near her.

Many women feel in some way responsible for the injuries they have received from violent partners and attempt to avoid 'provoking' their partners by becoming extremely sensitive to issues which may anger the men and by 'walking on eggshells'. This is not the kind of self- protective action we mean when we encourage women to take steps to increase their safety. We always try to make the distinction clear in our conversations with women. Our aim is to be flexible, seeing some couples together, others individually, depending upon the level of motivation expressed by the man involved to work on controlling his violence and the level of risk with which the woman appears to be living. If there is any doubt about the level of risk, we would offer a woman an individual appointment.

One woman's perspective on risk

Nina, an Afro-Caribbean woman in her late twenties, was first seen together with her partner, Ben, for help with marital problems. It quickly became clear that severe violence was a long-standing problem. Her partner was offered individual therapy with the goal of learning to control his aggressive behaviour. In a departure from usual solution focused practice, this goal was a precondition for therapy. Nina was offered individual sessions with another therapist, a woman, to find out what, if anything, she wanted from therapy. The therapist decided to explore with her what she might do to improve her chances of safety. This too was a departure from a purely solution focused approach, with the therapist putting safety on the agenda.

Therapist I notice you still... (indicates Nina's black eye)
Nina Yes, it's still...a week ago.
Therapist (nods) So things have been feeling very unsafe?
Nina Yes, that's Ben all over. If you don't see something his way, he lashes out.
Therapist Have there been times when you felt that could change...?
Nina I did in the beginning...then he started making me think it was

me...he's always got to have someone to blame for the way he is and his life...I thought, well maybe it might be me but I know it's not.

Therapist Well, he's been coming here for help in controlling his violence and I guess if there's a side of things that you might be expected to look after, it wouldn't be his violence, it would be your safety.

Nina He can't argue...I don't argue with him anymore. I haven't argued with him in over a year because it doesn't matter what you say, (in his view) you're either trying to pacify him or trying to wind him up...

Nina went on to describe in detail past violent incidents and her attempts to avoid 'provoking' Ben.

Therapist It sounds as though you're trying to keep the peace.

Nina I can't really be bothered...I've more or less had enough.

Therapist What would it take for you and the children to feel safe?

Nina I don't know because when he's been away from us in the past I've had him coming round at all hours so when we're apart its no better...we're always going to live in fear (close to tears)... walking on eggshells with him. You have to keep one step ahead.

Therapist So, in that you're trying to keep one step ahead, you've got those fears, what steps do you think of taking to keep yourself and your children safe?

Nina I don't take any steps. I just get numb. My mind goes blank. My mum says just run, get the kids and run... fortunately the kids weren't there the last time but I just won't run.

Therapist I also think it's very difficult advice to take. It's easy for outsiders to say (leave)... I guess when people stay together even through terrible times that some of the time you feel the two of you feel you have something going for you.

Nina My feelings for him are numb, I don't feel anything now... I don't want to talk to him because I remember last week (indicates black eye). For him it's like nothing happened.

Therapist But you know that it's happened.

Nina The bad times outweigh the good times...I'd rather just make a

clean break but you can't say something like that to Ben...I find
I have to think, how will he take that?

Therapist If things could work out the way you want them to, never
mind his opinion for a moment, because I think you already
spend a lot of time putting yourself in his shoes and imagining
what he's going to say or think, if things could work out the way
you want, how would that be?

Nina I just want peace of mind to know I can say whatever comes out
and no-one read anything into it, just be myself, because I
haven't been myself for a few years... I just want peace of mind...
Last time we split it was about six months or so (smiles, face
relaxes). It was good.

Nina outlined the differences which "peace of mind" represented. She
imagined her children relaxing and being able to leave the house without worrying about her. Although she did not think they were at direct
risk of violence from Ben, she felt they suffered when they saw her
being beaten or threatened with weapons. The team phoned through
a message to give to Nina.

Therapist My colleagues admire your ambitions for your children and
the wishes you have for the kind of mother you want to be and
we all feel that it's incredibly important that you live to be able to
do that and it sounds as though at times there are very real
threats.

Nina Oh there is.

Therapist I don't want to imply by my next question that you're in any
way to blame for what he does to you... what he does is his
responsibility and that's on the agenda for the sessions he has
with his therapist... if you're living with someone who's capable
of violence and who's treated you violently, you want to take
some action to protect yourself.

Nina Yeah.

The therapist asked Nina for a rating of her situation on a scale from
nought to ten of safety, with nought meaning least safe, ten completely safe. It emerged that she felt extremely vulnerable and that she had

done next to nothing to improve her own chances of safety.

The rest of the session was devoted to exploring possible ways of Nina moving up the scale of safety, including making use of her family and neighbours as allies. It became clear that she wanted a separation from Ben but did not want to relinquish her home, as many members of her family and friends had tried to persuade her. At that stage she could not imagine a separation occurring without further violence first. After the break, the following feedback was given:

Therapist We had a long discussion because you gave us some very serious and important things to think about…We all wanted to say how much we admire the strength of your spirit because it seems amazing how that comes shining through even when you're talking about experiences that have been terrible for you and the children.

Nina I won't allow myself to live in fear. (smiles)

Therapist You said very forcefully that you don't see yourself as a victim and in a way I'm tempted to see you as someone who could be a bit of a heroine.

Nina (laughs)

Therapist But I'm also feeling that sometimes heroines can come to grief and that I wouldn't like to see you get hurt any more.

Nina Mmm…

Therapist You were really telling me that your life has been in danger sometimes and I take that very seriously. You seem like someone of such potential and at the moment…

Nina Stagnant.

Therapist … and at times life is so fearful that it's really hard to think about anything and yet when you have the opportunity to think for yourself you can talk about that potential and about the things you would like to see for yourself and your children. You've shown a particular way to show your courage and much as I respect that courage I'm also recognising that the way you are showing your courage at the moment, you are being courageous up to the point you might even lose your children because I guess if something happened to you or to them they end up being looked after by Social Services and not by you.

Nina Mmm...

Therapist ... as one woman to another, I think there's nothing a woman can do that justifies male violence against her... so when you sometimes ask yourself, "Is it something I'm doing?"...

Nina (shaking head) I did in the past but not anymore.

Therapist So it's not deserved and it's not justified...Although there's no justification for male violence, I think women have a responsibility to do all that is in their power to keep themselves safe. You know I would say that about myself too?

Nina Yeah

Therapist ...I guess a lot of people who would like to see you safe are saying "Move out! Just get out of this terrible danger you're in", and so I'm not going to argue with you because I think your decision has to be respected. You've decided to show your courage in that particular way and so I'd like to suggest that you start to notice those actions, even as you stay, that can increase your safety and that of your children even if only by half a percent, actions that you are taking, people who can contribute to your safety and theirs.

The therapist faced a dilemma in wishing to encourage Nina to take steps to improve her safety at the same time as needing to avoid attempting to convince her in ways which had proved ineffective when tried by other people. While the therapist believed, at that point, that separating from Ben was Nina's best chance of escaping further violence, or even the threat of death, she recognized that trying to persuade her to consider that option was unlikely to succeed. Her approach was therefore to attempt to open up a range of possibilities for Nina without trying to persuade her as others had already tried and failed to do.

Several months after this session, Nina and Ben separated. He managed to handle the situation in a calmer way than in the past and did nothing to intimidate or threaten Nina. They reunited after about six months, once Nina felt confident that Ben had learnt to keep his temper under control.

Declining the invitation to full responsibility.
Jason and Wendy, a white British couple in their late twenties, had separated for the third time after Jason beat Wendy. Their other separa-
tions had followed threatening incidents. Wendy sought help for their
two children who had been distressed by seeing their mother hurt and
who were finding it hard to adjust to the separation and access visits by
their father. After Wendy and the children had been seen, Jason was
offered an appointment with a view to hearing his views and consid-
ering possible ways to help the children to cope. It quickly became
clear that he wanted to get back with Wendy. He was seen two to three
months after he and Wendy separated. I attempted to explore the
extent to which he was willing to accept responsibility for his violent
actions and to work on controlling violence in future.

Therapist How often are you getting to see the children?
Jason Every day.
Therapist Is that something that's increased?
Jason (nods) Yes, I see all of them every day, trying to get things back
    together and build it up again.

Jason explained that he and Wendy had not had any rows since he
left the family home. He attributed this change to the fact that they
were "not getting under one another's feet" since living apart and
that he had stopped drinking alcohol. He asserted that he could not
control his temper when he had been drinking and that therefore giving up alcohol was a major step in the right direction for him to get
back with Wendy.
    When asked what else he would have to do to keep his temper
under control, apart from giving up drinking, he did not have any
ideas. Worryingly, he described the ways in which he lost his temper
with inanimate objects when he was unable to make them work, for
example when engaged in Do It Yourself activities around the house.
While saying that he would not react in a similarly violently way
toward his partner or children, he implied that smashing things was
beyond his control at times. Although smashing objects was obviously likely to upset and intimidate Wendy and the children, he did
not appear interested in gaining control over that expression of

anger. He seemed to see smashing things as a solution to feelings of anger or frustration.

Therapist I have the impression there have been times in the past when Wendy has been quite scared of you. Is that fair to say? I think I've understood that right.

Jason Yeah.

Therapist Are you happy with that or would you prefer it to be different?

Jason No, I'm not happy with it...She's always thought I was going to hit her even when I was nice to her, so in the end, I did.

Therapist How confident are you that's not going to happen again?

Jason Well, I didn't want it to happen that time. Soon as I'd done it, I said sorry. I didn't mean to do it.

Therapist How do you think it happened?

Jason Spur of the moment.

Therapist If that happened, if you were in that situation again...?

Jason See, I was drinking, see, I can't control myself. Once I'm not drinking, I can control my mind.

Therapist So, say you're in a situation where you're getting angry but you're not drinking, how would you -

Jason Shout.

Therapist O.K., Mmm...

Jason Louder she got, louder I'd get and then in the end, she'd crack.

Therapist And is that the way you expect you'll be dealing with your differences of opinion in the future or -?

Jason No...we just walk away from each other now, that's it, just ignore it like. Sometimes we snap at each other...

Therapist From your point of view, let's just invent a scale, where 0 is when you and Wendy were apart and things were the worst they'd ever been between the two of you, and 10 is you're back together, everyone is feeling safe, you're both confident that if there's an argument you'll walk away or you'll find some way to calm down and not upset or hurt anyone, let's call that 10. Where do you think you've got to?

Jason About half way. I wouldn't say we were all the way there yet.

Therapist So what's got you from 0 to half way? Let's review that because we're talking about a number of things that have helped.

Jason Giving up drink. Calming myself down's the next one.

Therapist And which ways have been the most powerful, of calming yourself down so far?

Jason Giving up drink.

Therapist (nods) Right, what else?

Jason I haven't a clue, I don't know, trying to be nice, I suppose. I need to keep control to keep the family...she's still afraid to have a go at me, but she hasn't got no need to be afraid of me. I know I hit her like but she hasn't got a need to be afraid of me, d'you know what I mean?

Therapist You sound pretty sure. Let's just do a rating again. 0 means you think probably you'll hit her again and 10 is you're completely confident you won't, where are you?

Jason About 9, near enough complete.

Therapist And yet she's not sure yet.

Jason No, she's not sure.

Therapist What do *you* know that she doesn't, about you? and the way you are trying to control yourself? Jason She's got the rest of her family telling her and everybody that I'll kick the shit out of her next time, slap the kids around, that's what they say. I take no notice of people like that.

Therapist What's going to convince her?

Jason They're all wrong, aren't they?

Therapist What's the thing that would prove them wrong? If she had a really tough go at you, verbally, and you held back...?

Jason I'd verbalize without hitting her.

Therapist Would that convince her you're not going to hit her, or would she still (worry)?

Jason No, she'd back down in the end.

Therapist So, she'd still be backing down because she feels that shouting can lead to hitting.

Jason Mmm...

Therapist Which isn't the same as being convinced there's going to be no hitting.

Jason That's right.

Therapist What would convince her to be as confident? What would it take for her to say "9, you won't hit me again"?

Jason I haven't a clue what it would take. I can only try my best, so if that ain't good enough, it has to sink, doesn't it?

Therapist You can know that you're trying your best but I'm wondering what would Wendy see that might give her a bit more confidence?

Jason Dunno.

Therapist ...I've asked you a lot of questions. Anything you want to ask me? Jason No - what do you think then? D'you reckon I can change?

Therapist Well, I'm impressed by the things you have already managed to change because some people find giving up drink really tough...and if you can put your choice as clearly as, "Well, it's the drink or the family", then it sounds as though you're making the choice in favour of your family pretty often. When it comes to controlling your temper, it sounds like you're confident you can do that at the times you think it's important but I would guess that from the point of view of the other members of your family, they might still go on being jumpy for some time and it makes me wonder whether in the long run you might want to work on some different way, say when you're doing things round the house, instead of smashing it because I would think anyone noticing you doing that would be frightened by it.

Jason Mmm...

Therapist I would guess you are someone who, if you decided one day "Right, well, I used to have the habit of smashing things but I don't do that any longer", that you could probably make that choice as clearly as you've made your other choices.

Jason Mmm...

Therapist ...One of the things we do here some of the time, is work with men who want to control their violence because it's quite a common problem, especially between husbands and wives and it's usually the husband, because he's bigger and stronger and more powerful or-

Jason (shifts in seat, nods)

Therapist -more intimidating too because he has a louder voice as well, who's the one who's needing to do that. So, if you're interested in doing that, that's something we can help with...

Jason I wouldn't mind getting over it.

This simple sentence seemed to sum up Jason's attitude to his situation. He would not mind improvements happening but there was a limit to the actions he was willing to take to bring that about. He did not take up the offer of help to learn to control violence. While I was convinced of Jason's commitment to his family and his desire to be back with Wendy, I doubted his interest in taking full responsibility for his actions or working to control his violence. I believe he was willing to attend an appointment with a therapist to demonstrate cooperation with his wife, in order to get her back, but not to engage in therapy to protect her from the risk of his violence in future. As long as he believed he stood a good chance of a reconciliation with Wendy, without accepting full responsibility, he would be unlikely to review his perspective. In such situations, a separation brought about by the woman is often required to enhance the motivation of the man to consider working to achieve greater self-control of violence. The separation may entail great material sacrifice by the woman and any children in her care, especially if their only possible escape route is a refuge for victims of violence.

"How can I be sure that non-violence will last?"

Mary and Frank, a couple in their mid-thirties, of white British and European descent respectively, had separated because of Frank's violence toward Mary. They had a son of 7 and a daughter of 4 who lived with Mary. The children saw their father every day. Both Mary and Frank wanted to live together again and to be sure that Frank would not be violent again. They appeared equally motivated to protect Mary by agreeing to live apart until it felt safe enough to move back together. Prior to entering therapy, Paul had taken responsibility for previous acts of violence, rather than blaming his partner or distancing himself from his own actions, as we find many men in his position do initially. This meant that it was not necessary to spend time giving him an 'invitation to responsibility'. They were seen together.

At the first meeting, Frank appeared somewhat apprehensive. I imagined that he might have expected to be confronted immediately about his history of hitting Mary and smashing up their home.

Instead he was asked about how he spent his time which led to a description of his attempts to set up a small business. I encouraged him to go into detail about his relationship with his business partner, bank manager and potential customers and to explain how he managed to to cope with the stresses and frustrations of the enterprise. A picture emerged of a man who was enthusiastic about his work, proud of his self-control in keeping his temper with his colleagues and who had developed some strategies for calming himself down in the work-place when necessary. Frank recognised that he could keep his temper in some contexts.

Our conversations focused on identifying the successful ways Frank already had to control his temper and impulses to be violent with a view to enabling him to use them at home. We also explored possible criteria for Mary and Frank to decide that it was safe to live together again. The absence of violence over a short period of time may be highly ambiguous. It may be achieved by the woman 'walking on egg shells', or by the man's attempts to avoid anger, rather than learning to respond non-violently when angry. There may be lack of opportunity because of supervision by others or by restricting time spent together. On the other hand, it may be a sign of genuine progress in control of violence by a previously violent man.

By the fourth session, Frank was, with Mary's approval, spending much of his time with his wife and children. There had been no violent incidents and he felt he had made good progress in controlling his temper.

Therapist It helps me to think in terms of figures. If we call when things were at their worst 0 and where you want to get to 10, where do you feel you have got to?

Mary It's just the possibility of Frank smashing things, that's my only worry.

Therapist Has that happened recently?

Mary No...you can't really tell - things are perfect at the moment, things are 10, but tomorrow it might not be.

Therapist Maybe I need to ask you in a slightly different way. If I ask you to rate your confidence, from 0 to 10, in things staying 'perfect', what would you say?

Mary 6.

Therapist What would take your confidence from 6 to 7?

Mary For us to argue. I think I would have to get angry with him because I don't do that very much...it's the fear of him getting really angry. I'm just thinking, there have been a couple of times when I've reacted more aggressively, so maybe that will get better.

It was then possible to explore with the couple, some safe ways of Mary putting Frank's ability to control his temper to the test, so that he could have the opportunity to demonstrate his capacity to respond in a non-violent way and thus enable Mary to feel more confident. While it continued to be Frank's responsibility to keep his aggression under control, Mary wanted the opportunity to assess the evidence that she and the children would be safe if he moved back into the family home.

Violence is a potentially stressful and challenging topic for any therapist. Solution Focused Brief Therapists working with victims and perpetrators of violence need to adapt their usual approach. It is not ethical to take a neutral approach to clients' goals in such cases. The goals of non-violence by the man and the safety of the woman have to be a precondition of therapy. However, it is possible to take a clear stance against aggressive behaviour without preaching at or confronting the man with a history of violence. The therapist can express acceptance for him as a person, acknowledge his impulses toward violence and invite him to take responsibility for controlling those impulses.

Chapter 7
"My female colleague wants me to say..."

All members of the Brief Therapy Project aim to take responsibility for raising gender issues; the burden does not lie with the women members alone. However as men and women we do have have different perspectives to share. In my experience, when consulting with my male colleagues I spend an almost equal amount of time raising issues they appear to have overlooked as I do giving them permission to be less politically correct than they might otherwise be.

Pre-Project change
My early impression of the Brief Therapy Project was that two things made it a particularly appealing place to work. Firstly, there was a strong sense of sharing common assumptions about the process of therapy and 'speaking the same language'. Secondly, all the members of the Project were sensitive to issues of gender, race and class. It was clear that Chris, Evan and Harvey frequently took responsibility for raising these topics, rather than leaving the task to Ann or to me. It was some years later when talking with Ann that I realised that my first impressions reflected some 'pre-Project change'.

What I found in my early contact with the Brief Therapy Project was a recognition of the relevance to mental health of gender, race and class, which had been hard won. Ann explained that several years previously the staff group of the Marlborough Family Service as a whole had undergone a period of self examination. Perturbed by the imbalance in relative influence of male and female staff in the Service, the women staff had started meeting together to explore ways of getting their voices heard. Although stressful, this challenge to the power status quo had had some success. The Marlborough also embarked on anti-racist training as staff made the connection between imbalances of power associated with gender and those associated with race. A particular effort was made to examine critically the experience of black women clients of the service.

Respectful listening

When preparing to write this chapter, I asked Ann about her experience of being the lone woman in the Brief Therapy Project for some time and her reactions to my arrival. In her account, Chris, Evan and Harvey emerged as the Founder Members of the project, dedicated to applying de Shazer's model of therapy rigorously. They took responsibility for organizing the project. Ann appeared more sceptical about the approach, with her strongest allegiance remaining to Structural Family Therapy.

She remembers needing courage at times to challenge the interpretation of the approach being followed by her male colleagues and to promote more respectful listening to clients and less interrupting by therapists. Listening versus interrupting, scepticism about the approach versus commitment to it, appear to have become somewhat polarized along gender lines. However, when working as part of the team behind the screen, she recalls her suggestions being listened to and her contributions acknowledged. Although we all feel we have learnt to interrupt less through experience with our clients, Ann appears early on to have laid the foundations for the more sensitive listening to clients which has gradually become part of our style of working.

Interestingly, Ann does not remember being consulted about my visit. She says she had often wished for another woman colleague. Sometimes she had found herself thinking "perhaps only men can think in this logical way", which seemed the prerequisite for following the approach. Categorizing my therapeutic style as "cool and unruffled" but of a different pace (fewer interruptions, more pauses) from her male colleagues, she reviewed her idea that it might be an essentially masculine approach. However she continued to be concerned about what she felt was a lack of emphasis on clients' emotions. Despite her contribution to the early development of the Project, she has continued to favour working primarily in a structural way, and being selective about which aspects of a solution focused approach might be incorporated in her contact with families.

Another perspective on male violence

I asked Chris, Evan and Harvey for their views about the specific contribution of female colleagues in the Brief Therapy Project and also for their opinions about differences in therapeutic style which they felt might be attributed to gender. All emphasized the value of working with a woman colleague when dealing with cases of male violence toward women. Evan appreciated that when he was working with a man who had been violent to his partner, I had been able to see the man's wife individually. This had enabled her perspective to be acknowledged in a way which had been impossible in joint work with the couple and which she seemed unlikely to share with a male therapist.

Chris recalled a consultation break with me during a session he had been having with a man with a history of violence. The session had worried him a great deal and made him want to distance himself from the man's actions and attitude to his partner. He was in a dilemma about what feedback to give as he wanted to convey a strong opposition to violence against women without preaching at his client. I said I thought it was more important for the man to become non- violent than to learn to voice non-violent politically correct views. From Chris's description of his conversation with the client, the latter was less likely than the former anyway. Together we put each possible element of feedback to the test: "Is this going to be helpful in making him interested in working toward non violence?" A strongly worded moral statement against male violence was dropped on the grounds that it was unlikely to be helpful. I suggested that Chris's position on violence would be better conveyed by feedback that affirmed the importance of getting to grips with violent impulses in the future, than by a statement condemning past acts and attitudes. He found this pragmatic approach helpful in choosing words which avoided collusion with the man without alienating him.

Harvey has watched tapes of some of my conversations with men about their violence (see Chapter 7). He contrasted what he sees as my subtle style of challenging violence with his own more direct, even confrontational approach. He pointed out that I tend to use rating scales as a means to convey the desirability of change, introduce the woman victim's perspective and assess risk. For example I have asked a client which changes his partner would need to see before she felt reassured that he would not intimidate or harm her again and then asked for a series of ratings.

"With 0 meaning you have made none of these changes, 10 you

have made all of them, how would you rate yourself at present?"

"How would your partner rate you?"

"On a scale from 0, meaning no interest in making further changes to 10, you would do anything to make the changes, how would you rate your interest in changing in these ways?"

"How confident are you you can make sufficient changes to enable your partner to be sure of her safety? With 0 meaning no confidence whatsoever and 10 total confidence, how do you rate yourself?"

As with Chris's feedback, I think comments and questions, which make an anti-violence stance clear and which emphasize the violent man's responsibility for controlling aggression, are often more helpful than statements of confrontation or condemnation.

It is not surprising that violence featured in our conversations about working together. I think we all continue to find it one of the most difficult issues with which to work and all need to seek one another's opinions on particular pieces of work. It makes sense to have a balance of male and female perspectives when working with perpe-trators and victims of violence. Each gender carries strengths and vul-nerabilities into the work.

While men may be able to join with male clients more readily, they run the risk of appearing to collude with unacceptable actions or atti-tudes. Whereas violent men may prefer, as many men do, to confide in a woman, a woman therapist may fall into the trap of 'walking on eggshells' to avoid stirring up any angry feelings during a conversation with a client who has a history of violence. A female therapist may be seen by a client who has been the victim of violence as more likely to be sympathetic, while she may also be perceived as powerless in the same way the client has felt powerless. Male therapists have the advan-tage of presenting, to women clients, the perspective of a man opposed to violence but may become idealised by clients who have been victims. Just as Chris, Evan and Harvey appreciate the contribution of their female colleagues in this challenging area, I have found their support and ideas invaluable in developing skills with these clients. Moreover, I think I might have shied away from the subject had I not had the opportunity to collaborate with them.

Child sexual abuse

The main way in which Ann and I have contributed to the Brief Therapy Project's work with clients who have been sexually abused in the past is to see women clients who have expressed a preference for a female therapist. However not all women do express a preference and some who have been receiving therapy to help resolve another problem have disclosed abuse to a male therapist and chosen to continue working with him. I was part of Harvey's team in such a case.

Paula, a white British woman in her forties, had clearly found talking with Harvey helpful and wanted similar help for the problems which had plagued her since being sexually abused in childhood. However, he felt apprehensive that, as a man, he might do or say something during therapy which might be insensitive and which Paula might experience as abusive. In contrast to his usual active and inspiring conversational style, the first interview following Paula's disclosure seemed hesitant and problem focused. I had the sense that the client was going around in repetitive cycles of descriptions of her feelings which Harvey, out of respect for her and her suffering, did not feel he could interrupt.

I telephoned to ask him to ask her whether talking about her feelings had been helpful, whether she would find it helpful to continue, and if not, could he have her permission to interrupt from time to time to ask questions. Paula replied that she was sure Harvey had heard enough to understand how distressed she was and that she would prefer him to try to help her to find ways to cope. As in past sessions, she would welcome his questions and comments. Harvey could then use his usual skills to help Paula. In the break I joked with him that he had been running the risk of discriminating against a female victim of abuse by denying her a solution focused approach.

Gender and consultation

Some of the observations I make when consulting to male colleagues could be common to any therapeutic setting. For example I felt uneasy watching a male therapist working with a couple during a discussion of the partners' sexual relationship. It seemed to me that being outnumbered by men might make the woman less free to voice her views and that the man's assumptions and wishes about sex might predominate. This perspective was fed back to the couple and an offer made of either individual opportunities for the woman to speak with a female therapist or joint work with the couple by a male and female therapist.

Observations often relate to the specific aspects of a solution focused approach, like self disclosure by the therapist or compliments. The same words of self disclosure can have very different meanings when uttered by a male or female therapist. Self disclosure is often a way, in therapy, as in other forms of conversation, of showing something in common with the person with whom one is talking. When a mother complains that she has been finding her child particularly demanding at night, a male therapist's reply that he has a child of a similar age who sometimes stays up half the night may be experienced as a supportive statement 'parent to parent'. However, there is a risk that far from being the statement of joining and normalizing that the therapist intended, his experience serves to remind the mother that her child's father is not as aware of his child as her therapist is of his and may even appear to minimize her experience.

Although the contrast is less marked, women therapists also need to be sensitive to the fact that clients may assume that their therapist's situation is very different from their own. I have sometimes encouraged colleagues to make differences as well as similarities explicit during such self disclosure. For example, "I have a child the same age who's sometimes up half the night, but when it's my turn to go to him I usually haven't been looking after him all day. I guess I'd have to multiply my experience several times over to get an idea of the demands you have been dealing with". The paying of compliments to a woman client by a male therapist is a potentially sensitive area, especially if compliments about appearance are of relevance to the resolution of a problem. Paying compliments from the team or from particular members of the team may help to reduce the ambiguity than might arise if a client felt a personal comment was flirtatious or otherwise inappropriate. For example:

"My women colleagues noticed that as you have been feeling happier, you have started to wear brighter colours. They asked me to ask you whether you feel this is significant and, if so, what you think you might choose to wear next as you move toward your goal?"

"One of my colleagues, who is a woman, pointed out that your well-groomed appearance makes a favourable impression of your confidence. She realises that you may not always have felt quite as confident as you look but feels you should know what a good impression you make"

"One of my colleagues, a woman, advised me that, in view of your experience with men, you might be suspicious of a compliment about your appearance from me. However she wanted me to say how much she admires the fact that you have obviously developed your own distinctive and attractive style of dress. You seem to have risen above the critical comments you endured in the past about your weight".

Gender is one among many differences between members of the Brief Therapy Project but a particularly salient one for a team interested in social justice and mental health. Although, for the purpose of writing this chapter, I asked my colleagues some direct questions about their experience of the contribution of women in the project, I am regularly alerted to what has been perceived as my perspective as a woman by the phrase "My female colleague wants me to say..." or "One of my colleagues behind the screen, a woman, felt that I should say to you..."

Chapter 8
You can get there from here

De Shazer has said that he would prefer to train as solution focused brief therapists individuals with no previous training in therapy. He argues that practitioners of other forms of therapy have so much to unlearn that novices are preferable. I strongly disagree with this view which I see as excessively problem focused. While I recognise it can be very unrewarding to teach reluctant trainees of brief therapy, for example therapists who have been sent on courses they would not have chosen for themselves, most therapists who seek training in the approach come with many existing strengths. The approach encourages therapists to attend to the resources clients bring to therapy. I think trainee therapists deserve parity with clients, in this respect, and should have their resources noted too. Some relevant concepts and skills are outlined below.

1. The traditional therapeutic virtues

Genuineness, warmth and empathy have a vital place in the approach. Clients are unlikely to trust therapists who lack these qualities. O'Hanlon has characterized a solution oriented style of reflecting back what clients say as 'Carl Rogers[53] with a twist'[52]. This may be seen as good news for Rogerian client centred therapists wishing to bring solutions into their work. Rogers's form of feedback is supportive and essentially neutral; for example, in response to a client who complains of being depressed all the time, "So, you feel depressed all the time". The 'twist' provided by O'Hanlon introduces the possibility that change may already have started and that the depression may not be all pervasive; for instance, "So you've been feeling depressed, seems like almost all the time". Anyone who has been trained and practised as a client centred counsellor will have a great deal of experience of sensitive and accurate listening to bring to a solution focused approach.

2. Do no harm

All therapists whatever their orientation need to employ sensitivity, common sense, and a recognition of the moral and legal context in which their work takes place, to avoid harming their clients or others. These qualities should provide newcomers to a solution focused approach with answers to some of the questions most commonly asked in workshops about the approach. For example, "Would you work with someone whose goal was to abuse children/rape women/drive dangerously and not feel bad about it?"; or, "Would you ever ask an exception question like 'When are the times you are not unhappy about your child's terminal illness?'" Certainly not. Therapists need to utilize the sensitivity that usually guides them away from unhelpful or inappropriate interventions if they fear that an unfamiliar set of ideas and techniques may run away with them.

3. Change, context, individual and family development
Systemic family therapists share a number of concepts with solution focused therapists. Their view of change as inevitable leads them to challenge both implicitly and explicitly their clients' sense of being stuck. Although they may at times become bogged down by notions of stasis, the ever shifting family life cycle lies at the centre of their perspective. Skills in reframimg difficulties in non- pathological language and in the context of the individual and family life cycle transfer readily when family therapists decide to explore solutions.

4. Interactional questions
Solution focused therapists try to get a picture of the social context of their clients' partial solutions to problems, goals and plans for change by asking questions about the perspectives of significant others in clients' lives. Therapists accustomed to asking circular questions and inviting clients to imagine what another might say or observe should feel comfortable with questions such as, "If your mother were here today, what do you think she would say she expected to notice as you move toward your goal?" Furthermore they will usually have been exercising their mental agility and imagination in ways which will make learning ingenious ways to ask about exceptions an enjoyable challenge.

5. Strengths, goals, ratings and outcome measures

As a clinical psychologist, I found the approach's emphasis on clear concrete goals, use of ratings and respect for measurable outcomes reassuringly familiar. The practice of taking stock of a client's strengths also reminded me of drawing up strengths/needs lists. At first sight it may be tempting to ask "Isn't it just Behavioural?" Of course, the approach is behavioural but it offers the chance for any Behavioural or Cognitive Behavioural Therapist to learn some new skills as well as to utilize some existing ones.

6. Tasks, rituals, hypnosis and stories

A few years ago I would have thought that task setting, encouragement of family or individual rituals and story telling were among the methods which an aspiring solution focused therapist should leave behind. This was at around the time I learned that de Shazer et al had stopped giving clients tasks. However other therapists in the field of solutions, notably Dolan, O'Hanlon and White have incorporated all or some of these elements into their approaches. Erickson's naturalistic style of hypnosis is a strong influence on both Dolan and O'Hanlon. The moral seems to be that it is wise not to be too hasty in attempting to unlearn any skill which has proved helpful in past therapy.

Diversity within a common framework

The framework I have presented for Solution Focused Brief Therapy is essentially that developed by De Shazer and colleagues plus some of the adaptations which have grown out of our use of the basic model and the influence of other therapists (cited in previous chapters). The framework is deceptively simple but provides enormous scope for therapeutic individuality, expression of personality and gender. The diversity of styles within the Brief Therapy Project exemplifies this. It is a little difficult to pin down because none of us is standing still. Chris, Evan, Harvey and I sometimes joke that we should attend one another's workshops to find out what ideas and practices we still hold in common.

Chris uses a lot of story telling with his clients and has introduced the innovation of solution focused role play with child clients. As far as I know, he is the only one of us so far to invite a family pet into a session. Ann uses the whole framework comparatively rarely now and spends relatively little time in the Project. She combines solution focused ideas, especially compliments, in her more structurally oriented work. She has been influenced by Berg's writing on the topic of 'Family Preservation'[54] in her contact with families in which there are children on the Child Protection Register.

I feel that rigorous clarity lightened with openness and humour is the hallmark of Harvey's style, both in his own utterances and in the way he facilitates clients' elucidation of their goals. Evan's style reflects his fascination with language. It shows the influence of White's ideas about helping clients to rewrite preferred versions of their life stories and Karl Tomm's technique of interviewing the 'internalized other'[55].

My own style? The reader may already have some impressions. Evan has described watching me work on one occasion, noticing that I said little but showed attention to detail in responding to the client's statements. He felt a little mystified about why I was asking what I was asking. However, he commented that somehow the client seemed to be moving in an increasingly solution focused direction throughout the conversation. I was surprised at the idea of being mysterious because I believe in demystifying the process of therapy as much as possible. Perhaps his observations reflect the minimal intervention by the therapist to which I aspire. If a client is 'talking solutions', I tend to intervene very little, other than to convey my support and enthusiasm for their initiatives.

Occasionally, my colleagues comment that I have suggested an intervention which owes more to the Mental Research Institute (M.R.I.) than to Milwaukee for its inspiration. This usually occurs when I have said that I feel a client should "do something different" rather than persist with an unsuccessful attempted solution. For an example, see the section entitled "Is that helpful to you?" in Chapter 5. While the M.R.I. approach is concerned mainly with discouraging clients' persistence in using unsuccessful strategies, I feel De Shazer often combines the messages "do something different" and "do more of what works". Chris, Evan and Harvey prefer to concentrate almost exclusively on the latter form of message, while I sometimes use both.

Women therapists' use of self in therapy and in therapy teams

I argued in Chapter 3 that there are features of Solution Focused Brief Therapy that are congruent with the style of conversation that is more common in women than in men. However it is a flexible model with other aspects which are more likely to appeal to men or to women who do not conform to the more common style of interaction expected of them. The role of the therapist is as a facilitator, assisting clients in the discovery of their own strengths and capacity to develop solutions to their problems. It is a role compatible with a supportive and self-effacing position, like many in which women find themselves in the work place. While, in my view, such a role is helpful and empowering to clients, it carries some risks for women outside the consulting room. For example it is easy for women to find themselves in a similarly supportive role in professional teams.

Although there are now a number of prominent women therapists in the field whose writing and teaching is widely known, the field is still dominated by men. This issue was raised at the conference 'Therapeutic Conversations' in 1992[56] and needs to remain on the agenda of therapy teams. While a low profile may be facilitating in therapy, I feel women therapists need to draw on other more assertive aspects of themselves in order to share leadership and influence more equally with men in this important growth area of therapy. While I shall continue to favour a low profile and minimal intervention in therapy I recognise that a higher profile is required to influence colleagues - hence this book.

A therapist's medicine bundle

There are many ways in which solution focused ideas can be used for supervision and self-review. I like the idea of therapists borrowing Dolan's technique of the medicine bundle to encapsulate all their assets, personal and professional which they feel contribute to their strengths as therapist. I enjoyed carrying out this exercise and would like to end this chapter, which seeks to celebrate the individual differences therapists can bring to a common solution focused framework, with details of some of the contents of my medicine bundle.

"Here's one I made earlier"
1. A celtic brooch of my grandmother's given to me by my mother. This serves as a reminder of that side of my family, and especially the women, who showed hidden strengths in later life which have frequently astonished the rest of the family as well as themselves. In my grandmother's case this included making the transition in her fifties from the West Coast of Scotland to Calcutta. This symbol stands for hope, flexibility and the capacity to surprise. I find it useful to notice these qualities in my clients as well as to savour them as my legacy.

2. A photograph of myself aged 3 "helping Daddy" and wielding an alarmingly large hammer. I have had an ambivalent relationship with this practical side of my nature. At times I have shied away from being down to earth. However I have learnt to love it when utilized in this most pragmatic of therapies.

3. A post card from the United States. This stands for the energy, imagination and irreverent use of language which characterizes many of the North American therapists whom I most admire. It acknowledges a great many encouraging, inspiring and humourous influences from the other side of the Atlantic.

4. A rare "Thank you" card from a family. This one is remarkable in including a list of the specific things they had found helpful as well as conveying the warmth and hope that was the hallmark of the family. I value it all the more for being from members of a family of an ethnic minority who had appeared to take pleasure in educating me about their culture. Like most therapists I relish a reminder of having "got it right".

5. A small mirror to represent my own experience of a brief period of consultation with a therapist to help me make a difficult personal decision. Never again shall I underestimate the sense of vulnerability and anxiety clients may feel in the waiting room nor the relief to be experienced as the result of a perceptive normalizing reframe.

6. A photograph of the members of the Brief Therapy Project, to symbolize all that I have learned in their company, the support I have

received and enthusiasm for the approach which I share with them. I do not actually carry such a photograph around with me but the memory of good experiences in the Project often sustains me through less supportive areas of my work. So, this talisman has already worked!

7. Something to represent my profession in which my confidence as a therapist has grown. The British Psychological Society still produces only ties for members. When, at last, the organization comes up with something suitable for women, a scarf perhaps, it can go in the bundle.

8. A symbol of chance. Luck plays a part in problems and sometimes in solutions. Although the way people cope with chance events is highly relevant, their luck is neither praise- nor blame-worthy in itself. I find it helpful to remember this and to tell clients sometimes, especially if they feel they have been to blame for chance events which have affected them. I have decided to keep the final symbol a secret, thus affirming both the value of self disclosure and the right to privacy.

And so, gentle reader...

When teaching I often hear the comment "But I already do that".

On a scale from 0 to 10, where 0 stands for a complete lack of a solution focused influence in your work, 10, as solution focused as you wish to be, how would you rate yourself?

What did you do to get from 0 to where you are now?

Perhaps you are already at 10. If not, what would you be doing differently when you reached that point on the scale?

What would your clients and colleagues notice?

What next step would you like to take in that direction?

References

1. Briscoe, M. 1982
Sex differences in psychological wellbeing
Psychological medicine, Monographs, Supplement 1

2. Westminster Pastoral Foundation Counselling Training Service, London
Personal communication Emma Ward

3. Broverman, I.K., Broverman, D.M., Clarkson, F.E., Rosenkrantz, P.S., and Vogel, S.R. 1970
Sex-role stereotype and clinical judgements of mental health
Journal of Consulting and Clinical Psychology 34(1) 1-7

4. Ussher, J. 1991
Women's Madness: Misogyny or Mental Illness? (Chapter 9)
Harvester Wheatsheaf

5. Chodorow, N. 1978
The Reproduction of Mothering: Psychoanalysis and the Sociology of Gender
University of California Press, Berkeley, California

6. Meichenbaum, D. 1977
Cognitive Behaviour Modification
Plenum Press, New York

7. Weakland, J.H., Fisch, R. Watzlawick, P. and Bodin, A.M. 1974
Brief therapy: focused problem resolution
Family Process, 13, 141-168

8. Nautts, P. 1986
Brief Therapy with Women.
M.R.I. Training Programme Workshop
San Francisco

9. De Shazer, S. 1985
Keys to Solution in Brief Therapy
W.W. Norton & Co., New York and London

10. De Shazer, S. 1988
Clues: Investigating Solutions in Brief Therapy
W.W. Norton & Co., New York and London

11. De Shazer, S. 1991
Putting Difference to Work
W.W. Norton, New York and London

12. George, E.; Iveson, C. and Ratner, H. 1990
Problem to Solution
BT Press, London

13. Berg, I.K. and Miller, S.D. 1992
Working with the Problem Drinker: a Solution Focused Approach
W.W. Norton & Co., New York and London

14. Lipchik, E. 1988
Interviewing with a constructive ear
Dulwich Centre Newsletter Winter 3-7
UK distributor: BT Press, London

15. Weiner-Davis, M. 1992
Divorce Busting
Simon and Shuster, New York

16. Watzlawick, P.; Weakland, J. and Fisch, R.   1974
Change: Principles of Problem Formation and Problem Resolution
W.W. Norton & Co., New York and London

17. Fisch,R.; Weakland, J. and Segal, L. 1982
The Tactics of Change: Doing Therapy Briefly
Jossey Bass, San Francisco and London

18. O'Hanlon, W.H. 1987
Taproots: Underlying Principles of Milton Erickson's Therapy and Hypnosis
W.W. Norton & Co., New York

19. Segal, L. 1985
The Dream of Reality: Heinz von Foerster's Constructivism
W.W. Norton & Co., New York and London

20. O'Hanlon, W.H. and Weiner-Davis 1989
In Search of Solutions: A New Direction in Psychotherapy
W.W. Norton & Co., New York and London

21. Hudson, P.O. and O'Hanlon, W.H. 1991
Rewriting Love Stories: Brief Marital Therapy
W.W. Norton & Co., New York and London

22. Cade, B. and O'Hanlon, W.H. 1993
A Brief Guide to Brief Therapy
W.W. Norton & Co., New York and London

23. Dolan, Y. 1991
Resolving Sexual Abuse: Solution-Focused Therapy and Ericksonian Hypnosis for Adult Survivors
W.W. Norton New York and London

24. Weakland, J. and Jordan, L. 1992
Working briefly with reluctant clients: child protective services as an example
Journal of Family Therapy 14(3) 231-254

25. Furman, B. and Ahola, T. 1992
Solution Talk: Hosting Therapeutic Conversations
W.W. Norton, New York and London

26. White, M. and Epston,D. 1990
Narrative Means to Therapeutic Ends
W.W. Norton & Co., New York and London

27. Epston, D. and White, M. 1992
Experience, Contradiction, Narrative and Imagination: Selected Papers of David Epston and Michael White 1989 - 1991
Dulwich Centre Publications, South Australia
UK distributor: BT Press, London

28. Foucault, M. 1973
The Birth of the Clinic: an Archaeology of Medical Perception
Tavistock, London

29. Geertz, C.1983
Local Knowledge: Further Essays in Interpretive Anthropology
Basic Books, New York

30. Geertz, C. 1986
Making experiences, authoring selves.
In V. Turner and E. Bruner (Eds.) *The Anthropology of Experience*
University of Illinois Press, Chicago

31. M. Durrant and C. White (Eds.) 1990
Ideas for Therapy with Sexual Abuse
Dulwich Centre Publications, South Australia
UK distributor: BT Press, London

32. Waldegrave, C. 1985
Mono-cultural, mono-class, and so called non-political family therapy.
Australia and New Zealand Journal of Family Therapy, 6:4, 197-200

33. Weiner-Davis, M., De Shazer, S., Gingerich, W. 1987
Constructing the therapeutic solution by building on pretreatment change: an exploratory study
Journal of Marital and Family Therapy, 13(4) 359-363

34. De Shazer, S. 1984
The death of resistance
Family Process. 23 11-17

35. Andersen, T. 1987
The reflecting team: dialogue and meta-dialogue in clinical work.
Family Process, 26,(4), 415-428

36. Kral,R. and Kowalski, K. 1985
After the miracle: the second stage in Solution Focused Brief
Therapy
Journal of Strategic and Systemic Therapies, 8, 73-76

37. Tannen, D. 1990
You Just Don't Understand: Women and Men in Conversation
Virago Press, London

38. White, M. 1991
Deconstruction and therapy
Dulwich Centre Newsletter, 3
UK distributor: BT Press, London

39. Hoffman, L. 1990
Constructing realities: an art of lenses
Family Process, 29, 1-12

40. Gilligan, C. 1982
In a Different Voice
Harvard University Press, Cambridge, Mass

41. Burck C. and Daniel, G. 1990
Feminism and strategic therapy: contradiction or complementarity
In R. Josef Perlberg and A.C. Miller Eds. *Gender and Power in Families*
Tavistock/Routledge, London and New York

42. White, M.1988/9
The externalizing of the problem and the reauthoring of lives and
relationships. *Dulwich Centre Newsletter, Summer,* Reprinted in
White, M. 1989 *Selected Papers*
Dulwich Centre Publications
UK distributor: BT Press, London

43. White, M. 1988
Saying Hullo again: the incorporation of the lost relationship in the resolution of grief
Dulwich Centre Newsletter, Spring,
Reprinted in **White, M. 1989**
Selected Papers
Dulwich Centre Publications
UK distributor: BT Press, London

44. Trowell, J. 1993
Individual psychotherapy
In M.E GARRALDA (Ed.) *Managing Children with Psychiatric Problems*
BMJ Publishing Group, London

45. Frosch, S. 1987
Issues for men working with sexually abused children
British Journal of Psychotherapy,3, 332-339

46. O'Hanlon, W.H. 1993
Frozen in time: therapy with adults abused as children
Workshop: Creating Possibilities (Day 2)
Organized by the Brief Therapy Practice, London

47. Kowalski, K. 1987
Overcoming the impact of child sexual abuse
Family Therapy Case Studies, 2(2), 13-18

48. Durrant, M. 1987
Therapy with young people who have been the victims of sexual assault
Family Therapy Case Studies, 2(1), 57-63

49. Lipchik, E. 1991
Spouse abuse: challenging the party line
Networker (May/June)

50. Goldner, V. 1990
Love and violence: gender paradoxes in volatile attachments
Family Process, 29(4), 343-364

51 Jenkins,A. 1990
Invitations to Responsibility: the Therapeutic Engagement of Men who are Violent and Abusive
Dulwich Centre Publications
UK distributor: BT Press, London

52 O'Hanlon, W.H. 1993
Possibility Therapy: a Respectful, Solution-Oriented, Collaborative Approach
Workshop: Creating Possibilities (Day 1)
Organized by the Brief Therapy Practice, London

53 Rogers, C. 1961
On Becoming a Person
Houghton Miflin, New York

54. Berg, I.K. (Ed. E. George) 1991
Family Preservation: a Brief Therapy Workbook
BT Press, London

55. Tomm, K. 1993
Interviewing the internalized "other"
Presentation at 5th World Family Therapy Congress
Amsterdam

56. Therapeutic Conversations 1992
Conference held in Tulsa, U.S.A.

BT Press Book list

Problem to Solution – Brief Therapy with Individuals and Families
Evan George, Chris Iveson and Harvey Ratner, foreword by Steve de Shazer   £7.50

Introduction to and illustration of a compelling new approach to problem-solving, based on de Shazer's work. It shows how many apparently chronic problems can be quickly and effectively solved by using the client's own aptitudes and strengths. A clear description of the approach and its central interest in exceptions, and how they form the basis of each client's own solution.

Whose Life? – Community Care of Older People and their Families
Chris Iveson   £7.95

New, sometimes disturbing, ideas to be used with a minority of clients who take up the majority of time. Illustrates the human &professional dilemmas facing those working with older people, with the stories of clients and their carers is a story of theory-building, particularly around the application of family therapy.

Moved to Tears, Moved to Action
Jane Lethem   £10.00

The author draws on her experience of Solution Focused Brief Therapy with women and their children to look at case studies through the lens of gender. She illustrates the ways in which its conversational style, emphasis on revealing hidden strengths and potential for tackling social injustice makes Solution Focused Brief Therapy particularly valuable for women.

Family Preservation - A Brief Therapy Workbook
Insoo Kim Berg, editor Evan George   £12.50

The author's work will change practice and will open new solutions for child protection workers who have become dissatisfied with a monitoring role and who are searching for ways to develop co-operation with their clients as a basis for building safety for children. Some chapter headings: What is family based service? / Defining the problem/ Developing cooperation / Setting goals & contracts / Useful questions and other interviewing ideas / Conducting a family session / Do something different / Violence in the family / Alcohol and drug abuse / Those "god-awful cases" / etc.

Creative Strategies for School Problems
Michael Durrant   £10.00

A practical book for school counsellors, support teachers, and those interested in effective intervention. Includes ideas, techniques, case examples, and resource material on ways to work with students who are not "motivated", thinking differently about assessment; how to encourage the school system to notice difference; building on the competence of frustrated teachers etc.

BT Press also distributes
Newsletters and Books from the Dulwich Centre

Newsletters 1993

Newsletter 1992 No. 3 & 4
Men's Ways of Being

Dichotomies in the making of men *Gregory Smith* / An interview with *Biff Ward* / Men's culture, the men's movement and the constitution of men's lives *Michael White* / A visit to the eagle who sees afar *Rob Hall* / Father and father on *Graham Harbord* / Healing the mother wound *Maggie Carey* / Perspectives on the men's movement *Maggie Carey* / A conversation with *Steve Golding* / The politics of gender *Ian Law*   Double issue £8.50

Newsletter 1993 No. 1
Colonisation & Family Therapy

Colonialism – Then and now / Residential schools – the pain and shame / In search of a 'Just Therapy' – the mid-island tribal council context / Pura pura tuku iho – the seed that has been passed down / Gender – the impact of western definitions of womanhood on other cultures / Behind the one-way mirror / The secular and the Spiritual – a collision of worlds *Carmel Tapping* / Resonances *April Boyd*   £5.50

Newsletter 1993 No. 2

Exploring stories of Lesbian experiences in therapy *Kathleen Stacy* / Heterosexual dominance in the world of therapy? *Daphne Hewson* / Don't leave mother in the waiting room *Margret Roberts* / Internalised other questioning of men who are violent *David Nylund & Victor Corsiglia* / Comments on 'Internalised other questioning' *Alan Jenkins* / Imaginary friends *David Epston* / The narrative job interview *Cassie Bullard & Don Clifton* / Acknowledging Karl Tomm *David Epston* / Homelands film review *Sarah Jones*   £5.50

Newsletter 1993 No. 3 & 4
Professional Sexual Abuse

Introduction *Ann Epston* / Empowering clients who have been abused by therapists *Sarah Calvert* / A survivor's long struggle for justice *Jeany Marshall & David Epston* / Moving from victim/survivor to "activityist" *Melissa Roberts-Henry* / When intimacy goes awry *Estelle Disch* / A case of therapist abuse of a patient *Rachel T. Hare-Mustin* / Toward collaboration & accountability *Dean Lobovits & Jennifer C. Freeman* / Response to 'Toward collaboration & accountability' *Anne Jauregui* / The ethics of dual relationships *Karl Tomm* / Common errors in treatment of victims/survivors *Gary Richard Schoener* / Betrayal – clergy sexual abuse & male survivors *Walter H. Bera* / A systems perspective on sexual exploitation of clients by professional helpers *William White*   Double issue £10

Dulwich Centre Newsletters   £5.50 each

Social Justice and Family Therapy   Postmodernism, Deconstruction & Therapy
Men's Experience of Men's Culture   Schizophrenia some Views & Experiences
Living with HIV and Aids   Dulwich Centre Newsletter 1992 No.1.

Dulwich Centre Books

Invitations to Responsibility – The therapeutic engagement of men who are violent and abusive   Alan Jenkins   £14.50

Developing models of intervention that assist abusive males, by helping them to accept responsibility for their actions, to cease abusive behaviours, and relate respectfully to others.

Collected Papers

David Epston   £10.00

Five years of therapeutic cases, written from a personal rather than an objective and scientific viewpoint, and self-consciously concerned with the problems of representation in writing.

Experience, Contradiction, Narrative & Imagination

Epston & White   £14.50

A wide-ranging collaboration, covering such subjects as ways of addressing guilt, childhood stealing, dying with AIDS, and self-specialisation.

Pickpockets on a Nudist Camp

Ben Furman & Tapani Ahola   £14.50

Towards a simplification of philosophical discourse surrounding family therapy, taking account of the effect of the observer, and the tyranny of language: "The point is in challenging our way of making sense of what's happening out there."

Selected Papers

Michael White   £10.00

A carefully chosen and representative collection of White's work, the themes of which reflect his interests in constructivism and post-modern thought.

Ideas for Therapy with Sexual Abuse

M. Durrant & C. White, Editors   £14.50

Reflecting the growing awareness of the prevalence of sexual abuse, and suggesting strategies and solutions for therapists that take account of the interaction-within-context approach.

Order by sending to **BT Press**, *17 Avenue Mansions, Finchley Road, London NW3 7AX.*

Make cheques payable to 'BT Press' (add 60p for postage & packing).